WITTGENSTEIN'S BEET
CLASSIC THOUGHT E

CW00671461

I do not want to give the impression that the use of large machines or of elaborate techniques is always justified; sometimes it contributes merely to the sense of self-importance of the investigator, and it is always salutary to remember Rutherford's 'We haven't got the the money, so we've got to think!'

R. V. Jones in the *Bulletin of the Institute of Physics* (1962) recalling the dictum of Ernest Rutherford

MARTIN COHEN

Wittgenstein's Beetle

and Other Classic Thought Experiments

Blackwell
Publishing

© 2005 by Martin Cohen

BLACKWELL PUBLISHING
350 Main Street, Malden, MA 02148-5020, USA
108 Cowley Road, Oxford OX4 1JF, UK
550 Swanston Street, Carlton, Victoria 3053, Australia

First published 2005 by Blackwell Publishing Ltd

Library of Congress Cataloging-in-Publication Data

Cohen, Martin, 1964–
    Wittgenstein's beetle and other classic thought experiments / Martin Cohen.
        p. cm.
    Includes bibliographical references and index.
        ISBN 1–4051–2191–2 (hardcover : alk. paper) — ISBN 1–4051–2192–0 (pbk. : alk. paper)   1. Thought experiments.   I. Title.

    BD265.C64 2004
    101—dc22

                                                                    2004010916

A catalogue record for this title is available from the British Library.

Set in 9½/12pt Walbaum
by Graphicraft Limited, Hong Kong
Printed and bound in the United Kingdom
by MPG Books Ltd, Bodmin, Cornwall

The publisher's policy is to use permanent paper from mills that operate a sustainable forestry policy, and which has been manufactured from pulp processed using acid-free and elementary chlorine-free practices. Furthermore, the publisher ensures that the text paper and cover board used have met acceptable environmental accreditation standards.

For further information on
Blackwell Publishing, visit our website:
http://www.blackwellpublishing.com

Contents

Contents

Notes for Experimenters

Figures

Forward!

This book is a collection of the 26 most interesting, if not the most useful, thought experiments (although some have indeed been very useful). It is no exaggeration to say that the whole of modern science is built upon the surprisingly modest foundations of half a dozen of the thought experiments included here. They are no more elementary, say, than Einstein's Theory of Relativity, or more complicated than, say, Sherlock Holmes at his most lucid. And in fact, in this collection, science, or natural philosophy, features more prominently than other sorts of philosophy. I make no apologies for that. (Well, maybe a small one.) But too often people have been turned away from science and mathematics and left to pursue interests in other areas denied, as it were, the appropriate equipment for their study. And equally, too many scientists – cosmologists, biologists, theoretical physicists – attempt to make sense of their hard data without the soft tools of philosophy: reflection and imagination. In the language of the writer and scientist, C. P. Snow, the two tribes need to share the same hut, otherwise one lot will get fat and lazy, and the others will freeze to death in the cold. (Which group will suffer which fate he does not say, but I like to think it is the philosophers who are getting fat and lazy.) Certainly blind science is merely technical happenstance, and ungrounded philosophy becomes another religion, something that speaks only of personal belief.

And this book is a history of a very powerful but still mysterious technique used by the great thinkers, philosophers and scientists for thousands of years. A history of theories about the world around us. Thought experiments are that special kind of theory that predicts particular consequences given certain initial starting points and conditions. Like experiments in the laboratory, they are tests devised either to explore intuitions about how the world works – or to destroy them. Actually, many real experiments are more open than that, from the 'randomly mix two chemicals together' variety favoured in poorly supervised chemistry classes to the unanticipated by-product of very serious but uninspired work. But there is nothing to say thought experiments cannot be similarly opportunistic. The characteristic thing about both real and thought experiments is that you control and limit the circumstances and conditions for the test, so as to pick out just one variable or one unknown. The key difference is that in the latter, everything is set out not in reality but merely in the imagination. The circumstances are described, not created, and the action is imagined, not witnessed. Still, in a strange sort of way, the thought experimenter is just as much a witness (in a well-constructed thought experiment) as any laboratory scientist. As one of the great thought experimenters (Plato) put it – people are put into the peculiar position of discovering things that seemed to have been there all the time, unrecognized or forgotten, in thoughts buried most deeply in the most mysterious recesses of the mind.

What will even the most diligent and attentive readers know at the end of the A–Z? Assuredly not how the universe works, nor even how to transfer brains between two people, let alone what to do if they were trapped in a trolley underground – with Hitler – about to run over either one famous writer or twenty 'Indians'... but perhaps they *will* know how to begin to frame such questions, and how to use a different way of thinking to come up with some different answers and certainly many new questions. Perhaps by the end, they will feel that they have cast off the shackles of the Cave (see experiment F) and rediscovered the remarkable power of the human mind. Perhaps, as is claimed for us by Roger-Pol Droit in experiment Q, the world will never be the same again.

On the other hand, perhaps it is time to stop talking about it and instead start thought experimenting. The reader is invited right here to jump straight into the experiments proper, and savour some of the excitement of conducting tests in the laboratory of the mind (as it has sometimes been put). The Introduction, 'Deep Thought' – essentially a brief history of the technique – may be left for later. But for those of a linear frame of mind, and for sure (whatever Edward de Bono might recommend) thought experiments, like all experiments, are necessarily conducted that way, it provides some additional background and ideas.

But for those of us with non-linear, downright disorderedly minds, an equally acceptable thing is to pick up the book and just read the odd experiment every now and then, preferably leaving a moment's pause between the description and the discussion. Because thought experimentation is about imagination, and harnessing its anarchic power in the service of understanding.

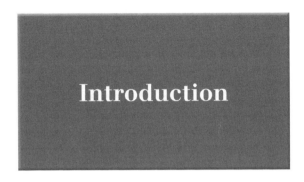

Introduction

Deep Thought: a brief history of thought experiments

On the face of it, thought experiments are a useful way to gain new knowledge about the world, by means of 'armchair philosophy' only. And, whether they are called thought experiments or not, the approach has had an important role in not only theoretical philosophy, but in practical science over the centuries.

The ancient Greeks particularly liked to explore using the technique. Not that they had no concept of more conventional experimentation too. Empedocles (495–435 BCE), who wisely divided the world between two forces, 'love' and 'strife', also founded one of the first medical schools, from which source a fragment of writing records a very practical investigation of the circulatory system. But Heraclitus (c.500 BCE), who liked to write in riddling epithets like the famous one about it being impossible to step into the same river twice, decided that as 'all is flux', it is ultimately by the power of the mind, which can contemplate 'what is not', rather than by senses forever limited to examining merely what is, that the truly important things can be found.

Ptolemy (87–150 CE), the inspiration of future mathematicians and geometers, as well as geographers and cosmologists, describes his homely view of the universe in the first book of the *Almagest*, and gives various arguments that sit somewhere between 'thought experiments' and real experiments. In particular, Ptolemy argues that since all bodies fall to the centre of the universe, the Earth must be fixed there at the centre, otherwise falling objects would not be seen to drop towards the centre of the Earth. Now his listeners could at this point have conducted their own 'real' experiments but it was clearly enough to reflect on their own underlying assumptions of

1

reality to agree with Ptolemy. Only the fact that the first assumption is rather a big (and rather a dubious) one stands between them and true knowledge, a fact that is certainly a reminder of the dangers of the thought experiment technique. But then again, it is also a reminder of the dangers of the 'thoughtless' experiment technique too. It was not the lack of testing that was a problem with Ptolemy's theory; it was the assumptions underlying it.

Another of Ptolemy's experiments is designed to show that the Earth must not only be at the centre of the universe, but completely motionless – steady as a rock – too. To do this, Ptolemy asks us to consider the fact that that if the Earth moved, as some earlier philosophers had suggested, then certain bizarre consequences would have to follow. In particular, if the Earth rotated once every 24 hours, was it not intuitively obvious that an object thrown vertically upwards would not fall back to the same place, but would fall back slightly to one side?

Ptolemy's record is not encouraging, but then his experiments were not truly thought ones. For Plato, as for Heraclitus, those wishing to understand phenomena in the natural world should recognize that experience of events is a poor guide. Plato's dialogues are littered (for want of a kinder term) with thought experiments. Alongside Gyges with his magic ring exploring the nature of morality is the 'mad friend' hunting for his knife; elsewhere there is Plato himself conducting the (less well known) 'breeding experiment' in which he advances the case for eugenics for the good of society; and over there is the much repeated but little agreed upon metaphor of the prisoners in the cave, that seems to be telling us something about the nature of knowledge. Less often appreciated, but still very influential, is that the entire process of the development of society outlined in the *Republic* is actually a carefully crafted thought experiment, built on the assumption that people will not be content with all the fruits of nature – but will want to eat meat, leading to a struggle for land and resources.

But it is in Plato's account of Socrates leading the slave boy, Meno, to develop the Pythagorean principle that new knowledge appears to emerge from introspection in the best manner of the technique. Many of the Ancients valued such 'pure' knowledge, quintessentially mathematical, more highly than any that relied on actually going out and looking at real things, and the notion of 'truths' waiting to be discovered by contemplation is appropriately sometimes dubbed 'Platonist'. Thought experimenters are his fellow travellers.

Even Aristotle, who like a certain kind of scientist usually maintained the supremacy of observation, tried one or two thought experiments. In his *Metaphysics* (Book VII, iii) for instance, he offers the experiment of two individuals, Plato and Socrates, having their 'non-essential' properties stripped away leaving only their 'essence'. How many essences are there, he asks? One or two?

But Aristotle's importance in the history of the technique lies less in his use of it than in his provision of a wealth of poorly judged and false beliefs about the physical world. As Bertrand Russell has pointed out, Aristotle, in spite of his reputation, is full of absurdities. For instance, Aristotle insists that the blood of females is blacker than that of males; that the pig is the only animal liable to measles; that an elephant suffering from insomnia should have its shoulders rubbed with salt, olive-oil and warm water; and that women have fewer teeth than men. But there have also been more weighty opinions about gravity, time and space that subsequent philosophers and scientists have had to labour mightily to demonstrate the error of. And often the most compelling refutations have been not empirical, but conceptual, using the thought experiment technique. (Although not, admittedly in the matter of numbers of teeth. There is still a place for observation.)

Medieval philosophers, for example, used the idea of a lance with a sharpened handle (that is, as well as a sharpened point) to disprove Aristotle's theory that things like lances only flew through the air when released, rather than falling bemusedly straight to the ground in shocked realization that they were no longer being held, by virtue of the 'pressure' of air rushing in behind them. (The air's ability to press on the sharpened handle did not seem to them likely to affect the lance.) The medievals particularly valued such thought experiments in their debating technique of 'challenges', which used all kinds of 'common sense' experiments to settle disputes. In a formalized process known as 'obligationes', disputants were 'obliged' to either assent, dissent or doubt statements, until such time as a 'contradiction' was demonstrated in one or the other's position. A double-pointed lance, although easy enough to produce to the court, was not necessary.

But it was the Renaissance that produced the richest crop of thought experiments, including those of Galileo, Descartes, Newton and Leibniz. These were thinkers whose interests lay in 'Natural Philosophy' and who considered that the best experiments work by making conscious and obvious what any assumed laws of nature really are. Descartes used the technique particularly enthusiastically, offering in his *Meditations* (1641) the original 'brain in a vat' scenario, along with a 'possible world' peopled by automata, another run by a 'malicious Demon' (along with the general philosophical problem of whether we might all be dreaming) and finally the solitary introspection in the celebrated Second Meditation. It is there he finds that he cannot even imagine thinking away thinking and so is led to the conclusion that the only certain thing is thought itself.

Descartes took it for granted that whatever can be imagined is possible, in some sense. Yet although this might appear to give the imagination extraordinary power, he also insists that mere mortals are bound forever to the laws of logic, unable to even imagine a world in which, say, 2 + 2 did not equal 4. (Although God, Descartes piously adds, is above these laws.) Thought experimenters who dare to suppose an illogicality enter dangerous waters in which, even if they manage to survive, any findings they may eventually return with are worthless. Yet just what is 'illogical'? In another experiment, Descartes says if you remove all the matter from a chamber, the walls would touch, therefore a vacuum is impossible. Perhaps then 'imagining the impossible' is not always so foolish a thing.

Hume, like Descartes, considered that 'conceivability' equals possibility and that things which cannot even be imagined definitely could not be possible:

> 'Tis an established maxim in metaphysics that whatever the mind clearly conceives includes the idea of possible existence, or in other words, that nothing we imagine is absolutely impossible. We can form the idea of a golden mountain, and from thence conclude that such a mountain may actually exist. We can form no idea of a mountain without a valley, and therefore regard it as impossible.

Sometimes (but, as we have already seen, quite erroneously), the philosophical examination of thought experiments is only traced back to the Danish scientist, Hans Christian Oersted (1777–1851). Oersted saw them as not so much concerned with predictions or substituting for measurement, but as a tool for arriving at a better understanding of nature. For him the value of the technique lay in first of all supposing some kind of 'law of nature' and then asking the experimenter to apply the law in a new – perplexing – setting. This was at a time when German philosophers such as Johann Fichte (who had chosen for himself the task of finding a transcendental explanation for consciousness) or Friedrich Schelling (nowadays hailed as the father of 'post-metaphysical thinking') were indulging in 'speculative philosophy'. Oersted himself has been said (perhaps like Kant too) to have been looking for 'a middle way' between blind laboratory science and fruitless metaphysical speculation.

Certainly, in the history of science, the thought experiment has to be acknowledged as a scientific method in its own right. Galileo did not actually drop balls off the leaning tower of Pisa – it was a thought experiment. (Despite what some may say today, see experiment G.) Similarly, Leibniz's procedure for refuting Descartes' Law of Collision does not require the rolling around of variously sized billiard balls; the thought experiment alone is rightly seen as settling the matter.

Although it is not perhaps a *very* interesting experiment, it is a good example of its kind. Descartes thought that if a smaller object hit a larger one it would rebound with equal speed, and that when a larger object collided with a smaller one, then the two would move off together (in a way that conserves the total quantity of motion). Leibniz, however, asks us to imagine a series of collisions, in which one ball starts by being smaller, but the ball it is hitting is shaved down imperceptibly until the first ball actually becomes slightly the larger. At this point, according to Descartes, the behaviour of the two balls radically changes. But it seems ridiculous to suppose that such a tiny change in the ball's mass could result in it one minute bouncing off, and the next propelling the other onward, so Leibniz seems to show that Descartes is wrong.

And much of modern physics is built not upon measurement but on thought experimentation. Einstein did not carry out measurements in a rapidly descending elevator, nor did Schrödinger actually put his cat into a box with a radioactive rock; all were sufficient in themselves just as hypotheticals. They are quite *possible* as practical exercises, but the point of a thought experiment is that it really would not help to carry it out: all the information that is necessary is already there, as it were, in the hidden recesses of consciousness. And in fact Galileo, Newton, Darwin and Einstein all used them to great effect to resolve, not just explore, complex issues and scientific debates. They conjured up scenarios, obliged others to follow the logic of the tale and ultimately accept their findings. These were quintessentially experiments that took place truly in the 'laboratory of the mind'.

Einstein, a past master, used the technique to imagine what it would be like to travel at the same speed as a light ray. If you were to run down a pier, he mused, as a big wave was coming in, then the watery wave would appear to you as a stationary lump in the water. What then, for an astronaut racing a light wave – would it too appear to be stationary (experiment U)? In another thought experiment, a physicist has been drugged and wakes up in a box being pulled steadily upwards by a rope. Into this box a beam of light is projected. The 'elevator' as it became known, is designed to demonstrate the equivalence of constant acceleration and gravitational field effects, by showing that the light ray will appear to bend in both cases. From such simple musings would come the special theory of relativity. As

Einstein wrote later, 'from the very beginning it appeared to me intuitively clear that, judged from the standpoint of such an observer, everything would have to happen according to the same laws as for an observer who (relative to the earth) was at rest. For how, otherwise, should the first observer know, i.e. be able to determine, that he is in a state of fast uniform motion?'

Some say all this is a little too good to be true. They worry that whilst the approach seems to offer the advantage, through being made up as you go along, of allowing extraneous detail and complications to be removed, it may equally in so doing cease to be relevant or accurate. As Wittgenstein put it, 'it is only in normal cases that the use of a word is clearly prescribed, we know, we are in no doubt, what to say in this or that case. The more absurd the case, the more doubtful it becomes.' If you imagine things differently from 'the way they are', he adds, then 'you can no longer imagine the application of certain concepts.' This sits a little uncomfortably alongside, of course, his own liberal use of the technique, including examples such as the one describing a man whose brain is removed by surgeons, and another where we are asked to imagine a world in which all human beings look exactly alike (compare with experiment I), not to forget numerous other, at least 'quasi', thought experiments supposedly highlighting aspects of language. Ones such as the comparison with the controls of the train engine, or the one with a map of a street accident, or most elaborately of all, the 'beetle' that everyone carries furtively around in a small box (see experiment W). But then Wittgenstein (or at least the 'later Wittgenstein' as aficionados put it) did believe that language is best undersood as a series of pictures, and his thought experiments are also, in their way, only the logical manifestation of that approach.

In any case, the accusation of 'abnormality' also sits rather uncomfortably alongside the rich history of mathematics, where impossible entities appear without so much as a raised eyebrow – be they dimensionless points, perfect circles, negative and irrational numbers or whatever. Mathematics is after all one of the main sources of thought experiments in a tradition stretching from the ancient philosophers up to the present day. Those proposed by Bertrand Russell, Gottlob Frege and others to resolve the so-called set paradox (a debate in which Wittgenstein himself was closely involved) are rightly recognized as central to both the philosophical and the mathematical debate. And here, in the concluding 'How to' guide, we consider mathematically (but only in the most elementary mathematics!) a kind of meta-thought experiment designed to show how the technique might quite legitimately conjure up 'new' information from old facts and established assertions.

In fact, mathematics and physics operate with different rules, and should be kept apart to some extent. Physics is empirical, based on measurement, but mathematics is based on 'axioms' that are assumed at the outset. Having said that, nowadays, physicists, if not philosophers, see even mathematical knowledge as provisional and flawed. Indeed, Einstein once wrote: 'as far as the propositions of mathematics refer to reality, they are not certain; and as far as they are certain, they do not refer to reality.'

But for some philosophers, uncertainty and provisional knowledge are always going to be a bad thing. Many would-be moral scientists, such as Utilitarians equipped with simple rules based on the maximization of happiness principle, worry that thought experimenters parade 'a succession of bizarre cases' which actually warp judgement. Far from investigating moral intuitions, as they may imagine they are doing, they are replacing complexities with simplicities, while always supposing that doing so makes no difference. One critic, Alisdair McIntyre, has also objected that ethical thought experiments are 'ahistorical' in that they are detached from their original origins and debates. Others have warned that the thought experiments become like a stage play in which we are asked to become actors trapped into endlessly repeating the same scenario, proving nothing. Marxists disparage 'soft escapism', and insist that philosophers stick to practical issues.

Still others object to the reliance on intuitions, and return to the age old concern of the relationship of 'conceivability' to 'possibility', the debate that used to feature so prominently in attempts to work out whether God really did exist. But the same concerns apply to more immediate questions raised by thought experimenters. For example, on a medical theme, at what point would a person cease to be alive if body parts were progressively taken away? Such experiments appear entirely conceivable, but perhaps it is an illusion of conceivability, an unwise and fruitless adventure into hypothesis. This is certainly what Ernst Mach, who used the technique himself, meant when he complained about Newton's famous 'Bucket' experiment (experiment N), a generally mundane account of a bucket on a rope in which, nonetheless, Newton surreptitiously imagines the whole of the universe away. As Mach commented drily: 'When experimenting in thought, it is permissible to modify unimportant circumstances in order to bring out new features in a given case, but it is not to be antecedently assumed that the universe is without influence on the phenomena in question.'

The most implacable enemy of the technique, however, has been a certain kind of traditional 'analytic' philosopher, apparently concerned that he or she is being encouraged to infer conclusions from 'intuitive reactions' rather than by a sound process of rational deduction. (Although funnily enough, another philosopher, Richard Rorty, has said that thought experiments are 'circular' because our beliefs determine what happens in them. Perhaps the concern is that the technique is stepping on the toes of analysis, as there the aim is to start by assuming something, examine it a bit, and then conclude with your initial assumption, having apparently forgotten that that is what it was. No *new* information can ever be obtained by 'analysis', as any logical pedant can tell you.)

Certainly it seems these days that many contemporary philosophers' main interest is in debunking the technique. Thus, a paper in the journal *Ethics* by Tamara Horowitz spills much ink in the cause of denying the hapless Warren Quinn the right to use the technique to draw conclusions about ethical values. His experiments revolved around some 'rescue dilemmas', the infamous imaginary underground trolleys packed with different assortments of people heading forever to various sorts of disaster. In Quinn's examples, the numbers of people being rescued (or run over) stay the same, but the circumstances and indeed the language used to describe them are varied. Horowitz points out that people are inclined to forgive unfortunate effects if they are described as incidental whilst condemning those in which the consequences are described more explicitly.

In some respects, this is only common sense, but to Tamara Horowitz it shows rather that responses to thought experiments in general, and ethical dilemmas in particular, will be influenced by the wording, or what is sometimes termed the 'framing', of the question. This at least is something we must be aware of both in considering other people's, and even more so in designing our own, thought experiments, and is a point we shall return to in the 'How to' section at the end of this book.

On the other hand, there is nothing in the technique that says the experimenter is not allowed to change the wording if in fact it is shown to be skewing the results. Moreover, in a stout (if still also somewhat wishy-washy) defence of the technique, in the *Journal of the Theory of Social Behaviour*, Francis Roberts argues that at least thought experiments allow for investigations to be carried out without 'disturbing the environment' in the process, while elsewhere Jonathan Dancy, in an account of 'The Role of Imaginary Cases in Ethics', says that they can be just as good as real examples, particularly when fleshed out with details, even if they suffer from 'a certain indeterminacy' not to be found in reality.

Such as in Franz Kafka's story, *Metamorphosis* (1915), which describes what it would be like to find you had woken up and your body had turned into that of a giant insect. If you believe in reincarnation, the possibility is quite real, of course, and in the story there is also a ready made 'mind-transfer' built in, of the kind that has spawned so much vigorous recent philosophical debate. Still, even ridiculous stories may tell us more about both our intuitions and assumptions, be they methodological or ethical, than those handcuffed to reality.

That was certainly the feeling of Charlotte Perkins Gilman, whose literary utopia *Herland* (published coincidentally in the same year as *Metamorphosis*) described how three male explorers stumble upon an all-female society in a distant part of the earth. Many generations earlier, this commune had become separated from the rest of the human race, with the men dying off. The society had evolved in a distinctively feminist way, organizing itself around raising children and living in harmony with its surroundings.

Originally published at the time of the Suffragettes in England and campaigns in Europe and America for women's equality, Charlotte Gilman's story is a vehicle for her view of male/female roles and behaviour, of motherhood, individuality, sexuality, and other topics as well. But more recent feminists have had their doubts too: that the approach utilizes a 'restrictive male form of thinking' that should instead be trained into a more holistic, inclusive and co-operative mode. Or that it elevates 'abstract principles over contextual solutions', as Carol Gilligan has put it.

This is a little unfair. One of the most celebrated of recent ethical thought experiments comes courtesy of Bernard Williams, in which he imagines a man, Jim, who arrives in the town square of a South American republic, to find 20 locals there, firmly tied up, and standing over them the Captain of the local militia. To Jim's alarm he declares that he has just quashed their rebellion and is going to shoot them. Unless, that is, perhaps Jim, as a distinguished visitor, would like to shoot the first one – in which case the rest can all go free.

This experiment is intended to challenge precisely that sort of 'elevation of abstract reason' (in this case, utilitarianism) and kind of 'contextless' thinking. In running the experiment we begin to doubt whether such matters can be swiftly resolved by calculating the 'amount of happiness' that results, and overcoming scruples in order to save the 19 unfortunates. We have also to consider whether, much as we might like to help, we would be able to justify to ourselves the sacrificing of the first one.

But in any case, other feminists recently have not been above using the approach themselves – and with some celebrity. Sissela Bok, in her book *Secrets: On the ethics of concealment and revelation*, used a thought experiment with four imaginary societies in order to examine the issues of secrecy and confidentiality in activities such as psychotherapy and spying. In experiment V we will see Judith Jarvis Thompson invent an 'unconscious violinist' to test assumptions over the ethics of abortion, this one of the most successful and fruitful of contemporary experiments. To join in the debate, Mary Anne Warren, for example, unplugged the violinist's unfortunate neighbour and asked for a volunteer instead, while Roger Wertheimer came up with a scenario asking what would people think if wombs were transparent.

And like the feminists, whatever their personal doubts, even the most analytical of philosophers have also been unable to keep off the thought experiments. The great German logician, Gottlob Frege, overcame any qualms to conjure up the possibility of a 'rational tribe' who had an 'alternative logic' before concluding, sadly, that such a tribe could no longer be counted as 'rational'. (For Frege, like his countryman Immanuel Kant, it was important to demonstrate that a rule of logic is binding on all of us, from whichever tribe.)

Amongst other more recent efforts are Peter Strawson's imaginary 'world of sounds' in which 'position' is determined in some complicated way by the gradually changing pitch of what is called the 'master-sound' (this is discussed further in the 'How to' guide) and Martin Hollis's strange village (strange, too, in its resemblance to one imagined earlier by Gottlob Frege) in which anthropologists struggle to translate their language for fear that 'the natives' may use a different kind of logic to our own. Then there's Brian Ellis who wondered whether if the universe had just one thing in it, which he calls 'e', perhaps hoping to nominate himself (Essence of Ellis), that object could still have 'quantitative' properties? How big, for example, can Essence of Ellis be considered to be, when there is nothing to compare it with? No measures or rulers, no trees, no nothing.

Or there is Anthony Quinton's (perhaps rather feeble) effort to imagine the mind of Winston Churchill in the body of a 6-year-old girl (with a view to countering the notion that certain character traits require certain physical prerequisites) and of course John Searle's Chinese Room. This last has become quite a regular both in mass media discussions and on the lecture circuit, and I myself have not shied away from offering a 'souped-up' version here as the second part of experiment R.

John Searle originally introduced his 'Chinese Room' thought experiment (then titled, 'Minds, Brains and Programs') with the explanation that 'one way to test any theory of mind is to ask oneself *what it would be like if* my mind actually worked on the principle that the theory says all minds work.' He hoped his experiment would persuade people to the opinion that theories of Artificial Intelligence that award computers human-like thinking skills are 'bunkum' or, at the very least, 'implausible'. Other analytic philosophers, however, while sharing this aim by and large, cannot accept the proof offered by a thought experiment anyway. One such, Daniel Dennett, objects that as the Chinese Room scenario is not an argument, it therefore cannot be 'sound'. Unsound, that is, in the sense that even if all the assumptions made in it were acceptable, no one would be logically bound to accept its conclusion. Of course, this cuts both ways: even if you found Searle's conclusion quite ridiculous, there is no logical reason in that to suspect either the assumptions or the method followed.

But while writing a special introduction to a new *Journal of Artificial Life*, Professor Dennett also observes that philosophers have always 'trafficked' (as he unkindly puts it) in thought experiments. These techniques, he noted, are 'notoriously inconclusive'. 'What "stands to reason" or is "obvious" in various complex scenarios is quite often more an artefact of the bias and limitations of philosopher's imagination than the dictate of *genuine logical insight*' he says. Yet even so, there is hope for the technique. Searle may turn on his swivel chair, but for Dennett at least *the computer* can make the philosophers' thought experiment worthwhile. By modelling hypotheses on computers Dennett sees the whole exercise as somehow validated. As he concludes: 'Philosophers who see this opportunity will want to leap into the field, at whatever level of abstraction suits their interests, and gird their conceptual loins with the simulational virtuosity of computers.'

Of course this is dreamy nonsense. Philosophers should leave computers, like video recorders and photocopiers, well alone. It is only worth mentioning here to show that even the most hard-nosed 'analytical' philosophers actually believe in the value of hypothesis making and testing – which is strictly speaking that most evil form of illogicality, inductive thinking. The thinking, some readers may recall, that led Bertrand Russell's unfortunate chicken to waddle down out of the coop expecting a handful of tasty grain on the day that the farmer was planning a special dinner . . .

Much of today's debate over the validity of thought experiments centres on this issue. The distinction is between a technique that can provide new knowledge and one that can only present old knowledge a new way. On the one side philosophers such as James Brown say thought experiments provide what they like to call *a priori* knowledge of natural phenomena, such as the mathematical entities or 'laws of nature' that mathematicians and physicists wrestle with, and which may or may not be 'out there' in the world of the Forms;

while on the other, philosophers like John Norton stoutly maintain any knowledge obtained from them is not new, not 'discovered', but merely disentangled from where it is already lurking (in the disorganization of the imperfectly logical mind).

In fact it was John Norton who once grandly defined thought experiments as arguments which:

1 posit hypothetical or counterfactual states of affairs and
2 invoke particulars irrelevant to the generality of the conclusion.

But grand though it sounds, to say that a thought experiment is 'hypothetical' is to say precisely nothing, whilst to add 'or counterfactual' is to play at words. In allowing something to be either counterfactual or factual we are not venturing very much. In fact, some thought experiments are counterfactual, but many others seek on the contrary to demonstrate some facet of reality through all the elements being entirely possible, if not necessarily plausible. This leaves only the observation that thought experiments include irrelevant details as the definition which seems (in a possibly interesting way) to be exhibiting precisely the fault that it claims of the thought experimenter.

As to that, consider Galileo's Ship argument (experiment S) with its cutesy details such as the fish that swim towards the front of their bowl or the butterflies that continue their flights indifferently towards every side. It is guilty on all counts. Yet it is also the basis for much of modern physics, and created a world in which dogmatic assertion began to weaken. Up until then, as a result of such arguments, the geocentric system was forcibly thrust upon all philosophers and scientists by theologians relying not only on the guidance of divine texts but the apparent certainties offered by 'science'. Yet, for Galileo, the approach of the thought experimenter offered more certainty and greater validity than any number of measurements or predictions (leaving well alone the untouchable authority of the scriptures).

And so, if even today those who follow in Aristotle's footsteps are baffled by the whole approach, it is perhaps only the more reason to revisit the great discoveries and debates of thousands of years of experimentation in the 'laboratory of the mind'.

The A–Z

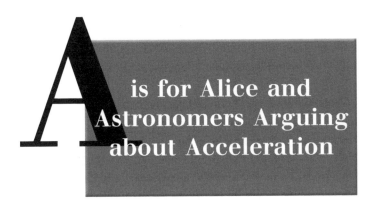

A is for Alice and Astronomers Arguing about Acceleration

SPECIAL EQUIPMENT NEEDED: orange marmalade

In *Alice in Wonderland*, Alice disappears at one point 'down the rabbit hole':

> The rabbit hole went straight on like a tunnel for some way, and then dipped suddenly down, so suddenly that Alice had not a moment to think about stopping herself before she found herself falling down a very deep well. Either the well was very deep, or she fell very slowly, for she had plenty of time as she went down to look about her and to wonder what was going to happen next. . . .

What happens next is that Alice famously (if implausibly) manages to grab a jar of orange marmalade as she tumbles

> Down, down, down. Would the fall NEVER come to an end! 'I wonder how many miles I've fallen by this time', she said aloud. 'I must be getting near the centre of the earth.'

But Alice keeps falling, now ruminating 'I wonder if I shall fall right THROUGH the earth!'

Like much of Lewis Carroll's imaginings, there is a bit more to the hole than first appears. In particular, in his day there was considerable interest in the plight of things that might happen to fall into a hole so deep that it went straight through the centre of the earth and out the other side. Not just ordinary people who might be expected to be concerned, farmers, hikers and the like, but celebrated thinkers,

15

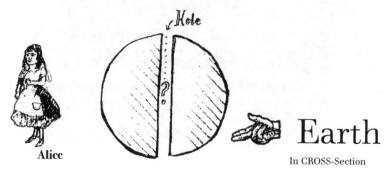

Figure 1 Alice and the hole through the Earth

including Plutarch, Francis Bacon* and Voltaire had found time to argue about it.

After all, for many years it had been believed that the centre of the Earth was also the centre of the universe, a mystical place where strange things might be expected to happen. Actually, the hole is a thought experiment *par excellence*, as Camille Flammarion might say: Flammarion, the French astronomer who produced a fantastical account of it for the *The Strand* magazine at the beginning of the twentieth century – with illustrations. (As Alice says, what's the use of a book without pictures or conversations?)

Now scientists might try to reach for a spade at this point, but they would of course be wasting their exertions. There is a question here, and it is best investigated instead in the 'laboratory of the mind'.

What would happen if something, say Alice, were to fall through a hole through the centre of the earth?

---

* Said Bacon: 'we see the iron in particular sympathy moveth to the lodestone; but yet if it exceed a certain quantity, it forsaketh the affection to the lodestone, and like a good patriot moveth to the earth, which is the region and country of massy bodies: so may we go forward, and see that water and massy bodies move to the centre of the earth; but rather than to suffer a divulsion in the continuance of nature, they will move upwards from the centre of the earth, forsaking their duty to the earth in regard to their duty to the world.'

Discussion

Galileo gives (at least) the correct mathematical answer in his *Dialogue on Massive Systems*. Such an object would indeed fall down the hole, its speed increasing all the time (neglecting air resistance, the earth's rotation and so on, as thought experiments are wont to do) until it reaches the centre of the earth.

However, although its speed would increase all the time as it is falling towards the centre, the rate of increase actually slows, dropping steadily as the object gets nearer and nearer the centre of the Earth, so that when it reaches that hallowed spot its acceleration has returned to zero. Yet because it is already travelling so fast (18,000 miles, 30,000 kilometres an hour) and the hole continues on, so does our falling Alice (or whatever) only now all the forces are acting to slow her down, and do so with increasing power, until when at last Alice pops out the other end of the hole through the centre of the earth – she falls straight back in again.

Lewis Carroll gives an interesting application of the principle in his book, *Sylvie and Bruno*. Here the German professor, Mein Herr, describes using a hole as a train tunnel to connect two cities a long way apart on the Earth's surface, the hole following the straightest route through the earth's crust (but not necessarily going very near the centre of the earth in this case). As the track runs perfectly straight from one town to another and as the middle of the tunnel is nearer the earth's centre than the entrances, the frictionless train (perhaps a 'maglev' one) relies only on gravity to run it smoothly downhill to the centre, acquiring *en route* enough momentum to carry it up the other half of the tunnel.

Curiouser and curiouser, such a train trip would take exactly the same time whichever two cities were connected in this way. Even trips bang through the centre of the Earth, like Sydney to London, would take no longer than little ones like, say from Paris to Moscow. In all cases the journey could be timetabled at just 43 minutes.

B is for Bernard's Body-Exchange Machine

SPECIAL EQUIPMENT NEEDED: **a body-exchange machine**

Dr Gibb – a dull, ugly, tweedy academic – has discovered there is a 'body-exchange machine' in the university science park. After some soul searching, he decides to give it a go. He enters one booth and transfers various elements of his mental capacities to Steve – a young, handsome and, frankly, not too bright, postgraduate student of his – in the second booth.

Steve thinks he is going to benefit by having some of his tutor's skills and knowledge implanted in him and is very excited. But in fact, Gibb has more sinister intentions. He wants to take over his young student's body entirely by re-programming it with all his mental attributes, and at the same time transfer poor Steve's mind to his own clapped out body. Amongst the options flashing on the control panel are ones to transfer all his skills, all his memories and even all his personal preferences and idiosyncrasies.

In a fiendish touch, to make matters worse, Gibb types in details setting out who the bill for the process should be sent to afterwards. As the bill is several millions, this is no laughing matter either. Of course, poor Steve cannot afford it – he might even end up in prison for not being able to pay.

Gibb is an utter rotter: he wants to do the selfish thing. He immediately starts typing in Steve's name and college address. But then he pauses. If he is transferring himself to Steve's body . . .

. . . *shouldn't he send the bill to the old Gibb, soon to have Steve's thoughts, rather than the new one in Steve's body?*

Discussion

There are many stories of body (or mind) transference – it is a staple of folk tales and science fiction, not just philosophy. Even Aristotle pondered the 'essence' of Socrates and Plato, wondering if in fact it might ultimately be the same thing, while John Locke used his pioneering tale of the Prince and the Cobbler, who wake up to find they have 'swapped' bodies, to show that 'identity' is really more to do with mental characteristics than with physical ones.

Yet the philosophical implications of the issue have still not been exhausted. Even if today science claims to have reduced both kinds of identity to the same thing. As the nineteenth-century physiologist, Emile Du Bois-Reymond, wrote:

> What conceivable connection is there between certain movements of certain atoms in my brain on one side, and on the other the original, undefinable, undeniable, facts: 'I feel pain, feel lust; I taste sweetness; smell the scent of roses, hear the sound of an organ, see redness?

It was to help explore this that Bernard Williams invented a body transfer machine which could be used to send knowledge, memories and thoughts from one person to another. He intended to settle the issue once and for all and finally say whether it is things like being good at discussing Kant, or things like being the hunky Captain of football, that give each of us our own 'personal identity'.

Actually, I have embellished Bernard's example slightly here. Now if the option selected had been to transfer all of Gibb's memories, skills and character, the thought experiment may make us think it shrewd, if unethical, of him to send the bill (and consequent prison sentence) to the old decrepit 'Gibb', with poor Steve's skills and memories. Meanwhile the 'real Gibb' would sneak off, scott free, in Steve's body. Such an approach fits the intuition that 'personal identity' is really to do with mental attributes, not physical ones. So that's clear.

But what would we think if the booth malfunctioned after sending Gibb's mental attributes to Steve, leaving them still intact in the original Gibb? Or if it simply erased all Gibb's mental attributes, leaving Steve disappointed at not getting any of his tutor's skills, but otherwise intact? Then we might feel sure there was still a real Gibb, one who was now defined just by his physical husk, and one who is doubly unfortunate to end up being bankrupted by the process.

C is for the Catholic Cannibal

SPECIAL EQUIPMENT NEEDED: **cooking pot**

Bertrand Russell introduces this weighty matter:

> Saint Thomas Aquinas, the official philosopher of the Catholic Church, discussed lengthily and seriously a very grave problem, which, I fear, modern theologians unduly neglect. He imagines a cannibal who has never eaten anything but human flesh, and whose father and mother before him had like propensities. Every particle of his body belongs rightfully to someone else. We cannot suppose that those who have been eaten by cannibals are to go short through all eternity. But, if not, what is left for the cannibal? How is he to be properly roasted in hell, if all his body is restored to its original owners? This is a puzzling question, as the Saint rightly perceives. (*History of Western Philosophy*)

In fact, this is one of the last – but not quite least – questions discussed by St Thomas in Book IV of the *Summa Contra Gentiles*. Here, as elsewhere, Thomas Aquinas examines the idea of a cannibal who eats nothing but people, the possibility of which had been used to challenge the Church's position in general and the theological doctrine of resurrection in particular. In the circumstances, rival claims such as that of Epicurus (around 300 BCE) that we need not fear death because we are merely a bunch of atoms and would be at least as happy dispersed after death as prior to it, presented quite a challenge to the power of the religious authorities.

For Catholics anyway, at the Day of Judgement bodies are resurrected from their old mortal matter. It is for that reason that God keeps track of 'every hair' on everyone's head. But for the cannibal, if all the atoms of his (or let us be modern, her) victims were 'returned' to their rightful owners, what would be left for the cannibal? The cannibal would either be deprived of the use of her body in heaven, or, as may seem more likely, excused the full horror of being roasted for eternity in hell.

So the problem of the cannibal family, as Aquinas saw, presented particularly (er . . .) grave difficulties.

What would happen to someone who had never, throughout their entire life, eaten anything but human flesh, and what's more (for the pedantic amongst us), whose parents had done likewise?

Discussion

'It would seem unfair to his victims that they should be deprived of their bodies at the last day as a consequence of his greed; yet, if not, what will be left to make up his body?' Russell goes on. 'I am happy to say that this difficulty which might at first sight seem insuperable, is triumphantly met.' The reason is that the identity of the body, St Thomas decides, is not dependent on the persistence of the same material particles after all. This is reasonable because, during life, by the mundane processes of eating and digesting, repair and decay, all the matter composing the body undergoes perpetual change. Both the cannibal and the eaten may, therefore receive the appropriate body at the resurrection, none of which need be composed of the same matter as was in their body either when they died or, for that matter, at any particular point earlier on in their lives. With this comforting thought we may, like Bertrand Russell, be tempted to end our discussion of the matter.

But ridiculous though the cannibal scenario may seem, the problem really affects all believers in life after death – not just cannibals and their dinners. As early as the closing years of the second century, if not before, the Church realized it had a problem, the one summed up by the Christian thinker, Athenagoras, as resulting from the reality that we are part of the food chain. After our death, our bodies will be eaten by a series of creatures some of whom, further along the chain, will be eaten by other humans. Since these later humans will share our matter, how will there be enough matter for all of us to be resurrected? The optimistic answer of Athenagoras was that human atoms are not (let us put this politely) 'assimilable' as food. But – to return to our cannibal family – that does not carry much conviction: why, the cannibals would be pitifully emaciated fellows if it were true!

A century after Athenagoras, another theologian, Origen, came up with a better solution. Resurrection requires not that we should have any of the same matter, but merely that we should have a body of exactly similar structure (apart from blemishes). Indeed, in the Afterlife, the matter should not be the same, since instead of flesh, we would have bodies made of pneuma, a mixture of air and fire. Using the same kind of language as Aristotle, who speaks of the body being driven by a soul 'as a horse is ridden by a rider', Origen says that we should expect a splendid new body merely modelled on the same form, not the same matter.

At this point, some too might recall Plato's dialogue *Phaedo*, where Socrates describes his expectation of 'life after death'. Socrates thinks

Figure 2 Cannibal and cooking pot

it will be a very good time: a time when, disembodied after execution, at last he will be truly free (from mortal concerns) to think and philosophize. Alas, later Aristotle would have none of it, writing that survival freed from the very physical workings of the body – the sensations of the eyes, the nose, the ears; the brain perceiving, desiring, thinking; the subconscious processes of a complex organism – must be an illusion.

And although Origen's 'same form' solution does seem to cut through many of the problems for the cannibal, he added a detail which would later be ridiculed by his theological *bête noir*, Bishop Methodius. Origen said that we would not need things like teeth, stomachs, hands or even feet in the next life. This seemed to him a very sensible thing to say, as such things get dirty or are generally distasteful. (Augustine himself was disgusted by the idea that we might still have to eat in heaven, and Origen specifically draws attention to Christ's saying that up there we would not even remember our spouses. That would surely be an enormous difference.) But if our bodies do not have all these bits, how could they have the same structure or form? That was Methodius' triumphant ('gotcha') question.

Perhaps a better way around it all would have been to assume that what survives the death of the body is a kind of metaphysical ego, a psychological construction. This was the conclusion reached by

Avicenna, the medieval Islamic philosopher, who argued that the body was only essential initially in order to create our identity. After that, identity does not depend on the body for its existence, nor is it even desirable for the 'identity' to inhabit a body.

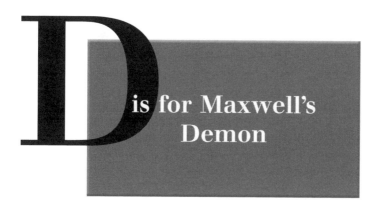

D is for Maxwell's Demon

SPECIAL EQUIPMENT NEEDED: **two chambers, one filled with warm air, one with cold, and a tiny demon**

In 1871 James Clerk Maxwell wanted to disprove the idea that it is impossible for heat to travel from a warmer to a cooler body without some sort of reciprocal change accompanying it. At the time, this notion was the basis of the Second Law of Thermodynamics.

Maxwell suggested that if a tiny demon sat at the edge of a tiny door between a vessel connecting two chambers, one filled with hot air and one with cold, and if the demon let every fast moving molecule of air that went towards the door from the cold through into the warm chamber, timing it so as to allow one of the slower moving ones to travel the other way, then in time, the temperature of the cooler vessel would drop and the temperature of the warmer one rise – all without any expenditure of 'work', and thus quite contrary to the Second Law.

But could the demon really do that?

Discussion

Indeed, yes. But Maxwell saw this as showing not so much that the law was false or at fault, but rather that it must merely be only statistically true. The 'law' still describes the world, but only as a matter of very high probability, not absolute necessity.

In similar fashion to Maxwell, the French physicist G. L. Gouy described how to construct a perpetual motion machine out of the apparently random motion of particles, for example, in a cloud of cigarette smoke. (The motion physicists call 'Brownian'.)

> Whatever idea one may have as to the cause that produces [the motion], it is no less certain that work is expended on these particles, and one can conceive a mechanism by which a portion of this work might become available. Imagine, for example, that one of these solid particles is suspended by a thread of diameter very small compared to its own, from a ratchet wheel; impulses in a certain direction make the wheel turn, and we can recover the work.
>
> This mechanism is clearly unrealisable, but there is no theoretical reason to prevent it from functioning. Work could be produced at the expense of the heat of the surrounding medium ... (*Note on Brownian Motion*, 1988)

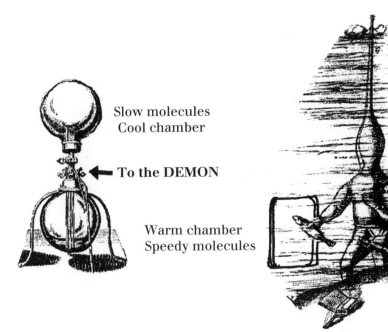

Slow molecules
Cool chamber

← To the DEMON

Warm chamber
Speedy molecules

Figure 3 Maxwell's demon

In fact, many other 'laws' are only statistically true – for example, the laws of economics are – but it seems too many people tend to imagine that somehow the laws of physics are as pure and certain as the axioms of geometry. The First Law certainly looks that way. Actually, worse than that, it seems that for some inexplicable reason the laws of thermodynamics are not even known outside of the scientific community. (As the writer and scientist C. P. Snow once remarked in a famous paper, 'The Two Cultures and the Scientific Revolution', 'humanists give a pitying chuckle at the news of scientists who have never read a major work of English literature, calling them ignorant specialists. Provoked, I have often asked how many of them could describe the Second Law of Thermodynamics. The response was cold: it was also negative. Yet I was asking about something which is about the equivalent . . .')

Anyway, the First Law of Thermodynamics is that the total amount of energy in the universe is constant, and all that ever happens is that it is transformed from one type (say coal) to another (say heat or light). And the Second Law, which the Demon plays around so diabolically with, is dismantling entropy, the notion that the disorder of the system cannot be reduced without outside intervention. (You can drop an egg on the floor and expect it to break, but not expect it to jump back together again.) Its overthrow is no small matter – effectively, entropy is the 'arrow of time', and the demon is a 'time lord'.

So *could* the demon really do that? Many have sought to forbid it, struggling to retain a sense of cosmic propriety, for example by arguing that collecting information about the velocities of particles is in itself work, so that the demon, for all its diabolical intent, is still respecting the Second Law. But I imagine the demon would laugh at them, sneering 'Easy peasy' as it *intuitively* opens and shuts the tiny door . . .

E is for Evolution and an Embarrassing Problem with it

SPECIAL EQUIPMENT NEEDED: **a planet suitable for supporting life**

Darwin asks 'Can the principle of selection, which we have seen is so potent in the hands of man, apply in nature?' Well, after some learned discussion of giraffes with long necks and so on, he goes on:

> In order to make it clear how, as I believe, natural selection acts, I must beg permission to give one or two imaginary illustrations. Let us take the case of a wolf which preys on various animals, securing some by craft, some by strength, some by fleetness; and let us suppose that the fleetest prey, a deer for instance, had from any change in the country increased in numbers, or that other prey had decreased in numbers, during the season of the year when the wolf is hardest pressed for food.

And now Darwin's answer is emphatic:

> I can under such circumstances see no reason to doubt that the swiftest and slimmest wolves would have the best chance of surviving, and so be preserved or selected. (*Origin of Species*, 1859)

Prejudice against fat wolves not substantiated. But there is a problem in Darwin's theory. Fleeming Jenkins, of Edinburgh University, at once pointed out that there is something dubious about the assumption that such traits could be passed on. Nature tends to 'iron out' individual differences, not to promote them. If the swiftest, slimmest wolf is a rare mutant, then that trait, however advantageous, will in fact die out as the inevitable result of interbreeding.

So, is evolution dead?

Discussion

In the later editions of the *Origin of Species*, Charles Darwin makes some small but significant changes. The emphasis shifts to the collective effect rather than the individual one. He now writes:

> under certain circumstances individual differences in the curvature or length of the proboscis etc., too slight to be appreciated by us might benefit a bee or other insect, so that certain individuals would be able to obtain their food more quickly than others, and the communities in which they belonged would flourish and throw off many swarms inheriting the same peculiarities.

So, struggle over. A thought experiment led Darwin to significantly change and improve his theory. In fact, it had to evolve in order to survive.

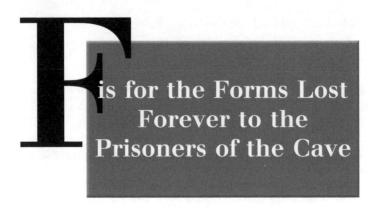

F is for the Forms Lost Forever to the Prisoners of the Cave

SPECIAL EQUIPMENT NEEDED: **shackles, bundles of wood, cave**

In Book VI of the *Republic*, Plato tells us about an underground cave, with a long tunnel leading upwards to the daylight. It is not a very nice cave. For in this cave are shackled a group of prisoners, sitting with their backs permanently to a fire. They have been chained up there as long as they can remember, able only to stare at the cave wall, on which the fire casts flickering shadows.

Now just behind them (but forever out of sight) is a path running between them and the fire. And from time to time, along this path, other cave dwellers trudge. Sometimes they are carrying objects made of wood or other bundles and so their shadows appear – to the prisoners – as strange, even monstrous, images cast upon the cave wall.

Some of the prisoners come to know and recognize the shadows. Both their own ones and even, or so they think, the shapes of giant deformed creatures. They give them special names, and credit themselves as great experts for recognizing them.

One time, a few of the prisoners manage to unshackle their chains and turn their heads, and see the real people toiling to and fro along the path. At first, it is painful for their eyes to look, dazzled, towards the fire and they quickly turn their eyes gratefully back to the dim shadow world of before. But on becoming more used to the light, they become able to make sense of the figures moving around and no longer heed the shadows being cast on the cave walls that their companions still spend all their time discussing and telling stories about. They now feel that these are misleading and illusory: even an obstacle to making sense of the world as revealed by their direct observations.

But when they try to tell the other prisoners that they now know the truth about the shadowy creatures, everyone thinks they have gone mad.

Unable to unshackle their companions, how can they convince them of the truth?

Discussion

Quite what the experiment shows is a matter of philosophical controversy. The background to this discussion is Plato's attempts to convince his friends of the reality of a pure and ideal world beyond our fallible and earth-bound senses. This is the world of ideas or concepts, or as it is normally put, 'Forms'. But I think it shows not so much that there 'is' a better world of Forms out there, but rather the more general truth that, just as the prisoners could be misled by being shackled underground, we could be too, and that it might be possible for a few wise people to have a clearer and better understanding of reality and yet be unable to communicate it to others.

Elsewhere in his most famous 'dialogue', the *Republic*, is a serious attempt to map out a new kind of society to be run by just such an enlightened few – the Philosopher Kings. Plato explains that what most people say in everyday life is beautiful, or cold, or green, or even 'a chair', is not really. The only real chair is the ideal one in the world not of the senses but of the Forms, the only truly beautiful thing is 'beauty' itself, and these are accessible only to the mind. And Plato goes on to say that those who are able to see the many beautiful things, yet not absolute beauty, or the many just things, yet not true justice, merely have opinions rather than true knowledge. Only the philosophers have this. Thus the thought experiment actually conceals quite a political barb.

G is for Galileo's Gravitational Balls

SPECIAL EQUIPMENT NEEDED: **balls, leaning tower**

One of the most famous experiments of them all was also one of the simplest. It involved the celebrated astronomer Galileo Galilei (1564–1642) climbing the leaning tower of Pisa, leaning over the parapet and dropping two balls, a large heavy one and a smaller lighter one, and watching to see which hit the ground first.

Galileo was thinking of one of Aristotle's laws, to wit:

> If a certain weight moves a particular distance in a particular time, a greater weight will move the same distance in a shorter time, and whatever is the proportion which the weights bear one to the other, so too the times will have to each other. For example if the half as heavy weight covers the distance in a certain time, a weight that is twice as heavy will cover the distance in one half the time. (*De Caelo*, Book I, vi, 274a)

So which ball did hit the ground first – and at what speed?

Discussion

For Aristotle at any rate, it looks like the long walk up the tower steps is overdue. But Galileo did not need to carry out the experiment. Instead, he ran the process through in his mind. There are only three possibilities. The balls fall at the same speed, the heavier ball falls faster than the light one, or the light one falls faster than the heavy one.

Yet suppose between the two balls we tie a piece of string?

Let's say heavy objects do fall faster than light ones. Then it seems the heavier weight will fall as in Figure 4, with the lighter weight acting, as it were, a bit like a parachute. So the two balls will together fall more slowly than the heavy weight would on its own.

On the other hand, once the two weights are tied together and held out over the parapet, they have effectively combined their weights, becoming one greater weight. Just holding the little weight, with the other dangling beneath, Galileo will feel this. When Galileo releases them, they must therefore fall even faster than the heavy weight would on its own. (Imagine the two are tied tightly together, for example, say by a single tight loop of string.)

It seems the two weights together must fall both faster and more slowly than before Galileo tied them together. And here is that thing philosophers love most of all: a contradiction. There is only one way to avoid it, and that is to assume that the heavy and light weights fall at the same speed.

Galileo describes the experiment as a conversation between two friends in *Discorsi e Dimostrazioni Matematiche* (1628).*

SALVIATI: If we take two bodies whose natural speeds are different, it is clear that on uniting the two, the more rapid one will be partly retarded by the slower, and the slower will be somewhat hastened by the swifter. Do you not agree with me in this opinion?

SIMPLICIO: You are unquestionably right.

SALVIATI: But if this is true, and if a large stone moves with a speed of, say, eight, while a smaller stone moves with a speed of four, then when they are united, the system will move with a speed of less than eight. Yet the two stones tied

---

* *Literally Mathematical Dialogues and Demonstrations*, although Galileo's paper is published in English as *Dialogues Concerning Two Natural Sciences* by Dover. Galileo should not be given too much credit for the experiment, which appears like many other 'Galilean' discoveries to have been borrowed without acknowledgement, in this case from Jan de Groot in 1586. Nevertheless, the style of Galileo's text is unmistakable.

This ONE trying to Fall Fast

This ONE trying to Fall Faster Still

Figure 4 Galileo's balls

together make a stone larger than that which before moved with a speed of eight: hence the heavier body now moves with less speed than the lighter, an effect which is contrary to your supposition. Thus you see how, from the assumption that the heavier body moves faster than the lighter one, I can infer that the heavier body moves more slowly...

And so, Simplicio, we must conclude therefore that large and small bodies move with the same speed, provided only that they are of the same specific gravity.

This is justifiably seen as one of the great thought experiments. Physicists know the principle that it established, that all bodies fall with the same acceleration irrespective of their mass and composition, as the Principle of Equivalence. It led directly to Einstein's General Theory of Relativity, which explains gravity by saying that when the Earth orbits the Sun, it is 'falling' through curved space-time.

Yet despite its historical significance, not all philosophers agree on what it shows. For example, in an ingenious paper entitled 'Thought Experiments in Scientific Reasoning', philosopher Andrew Irvine challenges Galileo's balls by denying that they can be really joined into one. Why, knots in the rope may come undone! 'The lesson of course is that thought experiments, despite their power and versatility, are simply fallible', he continues before concluding: 'Thought experiments, despite their advantages, can *never* replace observation and actual experiment.' Equally sadly, David Atkinson, a scientifically minded Dutch philosopher, concludes in his own paper on the subject, 'Experiments and Thought Experiments in Natural Science', that 'the new Galilean dogma concerning free fall is itself a non sequitur.' The conclusion does not follow from the premises. The roof is not attached to the walls . . .

This, for philosophers, is the worst possible insult. But Atkinson says that Galileo has brought it upon himself. He can be shown to be wrong and Aristotle vindicated by merely considering the possibility that, say, the leaning tower might have become submerged so that the balls being dropped were travelling through water and not through air. 'The situation is even more complicated when the terminal velocity is reached in a condition of turbulent fluid flow, as is often the case in practice', he adds in a flourish.

That Galileo may not have been intending his experiment to apply to a situation in which the balls travelled through a liquid, but rather in conditions approximating to 'frictionless', is swept aside as 'anything but self-evident'. Instead, the thought experiment's findings are exposed as only in some cases empirically (sniff) true, whilst in others empirically false. As for any notion that the thought experiment itself allows access to 'a Platonic realm of truth', that is particularly misguided. 'Galileo performed, and needed to perform, real experiments', Atkinson finishes loftily, thereby denying (like the Inquisition so many centuries before) the venerable astronomer even the right to philosophize.

H is for Hume's Shades

SPECIAL EQUIPMENT NEEDED: **colour chart**

David Hume brings us Golden Mountains and a world in which there is no pain, only varying degrees of happiness, as well as some rather more technical experiments in the area of business science. But we shall concentrate on his Blue Shades.

Suppose someone has seen many colours, but never one particular shade of blue. Then, says Hume:

> . . . let all the different shades of that colour, except that single one, be placed before him, descending gradually from the deepest to the lightest, and 'tis plain that he will perceive a blank, where the shade is wanting and will be sensible that there is a greater distance in that place betwixt the contiguous colours, than in any other.

And now is it not possible that they might 'raise up' to themselves the idea of that particular shade, even 'though it had never been conveyed to them by their senses'?

The experiment appears to destroy the theory that 'simple ideas', like 'blue', are necessarily 'obtained from experience', a theory which indeed reflected his own view. Hume, however, dismisses it all as too 'particular and singular' to be worth abandoning such an excellent general theory for.

But is Hume wearing blinkers instead?

Discussion

Hume seems to have had mixed feelings towards thought experiments. In particular, he seems to have wavered over when to reject implausible scenarios and when to embrace them. In his discussion 'Of the Balance of Trade', for example, he imagines four-fifths of all the country's money is annihilated overnight! A shocking supposition barely made better by supposing that another time the country's money multiplies five-fold. In both cases, reasons Hume, prices would simply change to reflect the amount of money, and so the change is perhaps not as interesting or dramatic as at first seems. These experiments led Hume to conclude that it is the amount of money in proportion to prices that is the significant thing, and consequently that a wise government will direct its attention more at promoting the welfare of its citizens and businesses and less at the 'protection' of its money. 'A government has great reason to preserve with care its people and manufactures. Its money, it may safely trust to the course of human affairs, without fear or jealousy.'

In similar vein, Hume supposes a world in which gold is annihilated. Immediately, he says, its role will be taken by some other precious metal, and if there were no suitable metals to be found, shiny beads or interesting shaped pebbles.*

But here is what Hume has to say about the 'Blue Shades' in Treatise I of *On Human Nature*. He starts with the lovely Golden Mountain, in order to demonstrate that all our ideas can be traced back to sense experience, before issuing his challenge.

> When we think of a golden mountain we only join two consistent ideas, gold, and mountain, with which we were formerly acquainted. A virtuous horse we can conceive; because, from our own feeling, we can conceive virtue; and this we may unite to the figure and shape of a horse, which is an animal familiar to us. In short, all the materials of

---

* Unfortunately Hume's discovery was not fully appreciated. As Bertrand Russell noted, at the end of the First World War, it was agreed that Germany should hand over large amounts of money to England and France, who in turn should pay vast sums to the United States. They failed to appreciate that money is no use unless it is used to buy goods. That as Russell puts it, 'as they would not use it in this way, it did no good to anyone. There was supposed to be some mystic virtue about gold that made it worth while to dig it up in the Transvaal and put it underground again in bank vaults in America. In the end, of course, the debtor countries had no more money, and, since they were not allowed to pay in goods, they went bankrupt. The Great Depression was the direct result of the surviving belief in the magical properties of gold.'

thinking are derived either from our outward or inward sentiment: the mixture and composition of these belongs alone to the mind and will. Or, to express myself in philosophical language, all our ideas or more feeble perceptions are copies of our impressions or more lively ones.

... Even those ideas which, at first view, seem the most wide of this origin, are found, upon a nearer scrutiny, to be derived from it. The idea of God, as meaning an infinitely intelligent, wise, and good Being, arises from reflecting on the operations of our own mind and augmenting, without limit, those qualities of goodness and wisdom. We may prosecute this enquiry to what length we please; where we shall always find, that every idea which we examine is copied from a similar impression. Those who would assert that this position is not universally true nor without exception, have only one method, and that an easy one, of refuting it: by producing that idea which, in their opinion, is not derived from this source. It will then be incumbent on us, if we would maintain our doctrine, to produce the impression, or lively perception, which corresponds to it.

Hume pauses here to restate the general point, using some dubious generalizations.

If it happen, from a defect of the organ, that a man is not susceptible of any species of sensation, we always find that he is as little susceptible of the correspondent ideas. A blind man can form no notion of colours; a deaf man of sounds. Restore either of them that sense in which he is deficient; by opening this new inlet for his sensations, you also open an inlet for the ideas; and he finds no difficulty in conceiving these objects.

That's leaving on one side the gentlemanly example of the 'Laplander or Negro' who 'has no notion of the relish of wine' or 'a man of mild manners' who can form 'no idea of inveterate revenge or cruelty', just as 'a selfish heart' cannot 'easily conceive the heights of friendship and generosity'. But now Hume proceeds to pick up his own earlier challenge.

There is, however, one contradictory phenomenon which may prove that it is not absolutely impossible for ideas to arise, independent of their correspondent impressions. I believe it will readily be allowed, that the several distinct ideas of colour, which enter by the eye, or those of sound, which are conveyed by the ear, are really different from each other; though, at the same time, resembling. Now if this be true of different colours, it must be no less so of the different shades of the same colour; and each shade produces a distinct idea, independent of the rest...

Hume's Shades

Suppose, therefore, a person to have enjoyed his sight for thirty years, and to have become perfectly acquainted with colours of all kinds except one particular shade of blue, for instance, which it never has been his fortune to meet with. Let all the different shades of that colour, except that single one, be placed before him, descending gradually from the deepest to the lightest; it is plain that he will perceive a blank, where that shade is wanting, and will be sensible that there is a greater distance in that place between the contiguous colours than in any other. Now I ask, whether it be possible for him, from his own imagination, to supply this deficiency, and raise up to himself the idea of that particular shade, though it had never been conveyed to him by his senses?

I believe there are few but will be of opinion that he can: and this may serve as a proof that the simple ideas are not always, in every instance, derived from the correspondent impressions; though this instance is so singular, that it is scarcely worth our observing, and does not merit that for it alone we should alter our general maxim.

This thought experiment, although much discussed, is really rather feeble. (The economics ones are more powerful.) We might (rashly) accept that each colour is its own concept – but why each shade? And what does it mean to speak of 'all' the shades of a colour? Even if we were to allow such a tidy notion, why should not a shade of a colour be assembled in exactly the same way as golden horses and virtuous mountains might be? Should we allow, as Hume says, that each shade produces a distinct idea, independent of the rest?

But Hume's own scepticism about the outcome of his thought experiment is rather revealing. Rather than dismantle his carefully constructed theory, having as it were ended up with one cog too many, he simply jettisons the offending instance. All quite contrary to what Thomas Kuhn would later advise good scientists to do. Kuhn it was who claimed in the twentieth century that the scientifc understanding of the world proceeds by fits and starts, as theories battle each other and perish when finally faced with irreconcilable contradictions. He says that far from our materialist world view being built up slowly and carefully, as the result of patient research and invention, each piece of knowledge fitting neatly with the rest, it lurches from one state to another – or undergoes 'paradigm shifts', as he put it in *The Structure of Scientific Revolutions.*

Actually, Kuhn saw thought experiments as fitting in very well with this approach, as within a good one it is possible to experience precisely that sort of 'paradigm shift' – where our assumptions have to be reconsidered. Perhaps forcing us (unlike David Hume) to adopt a whole new approach instead.

I

is for the Identity of Indiscernibles

SPECIAL EQUIPMENT NEEDED: **powdered wig, mirror**

Gottfried Leibniz, 'an elegant man in a powdered wig', as one wag put it, spent most of his life deep in philosophic contemplation, revealing himself to the world only through learned correspondences with several hundreds of other philosophers and scientists. Even so, his influence in seventeenth-century intellectual circles was great, much to the envy of Sir Isaac Newton, his rival for the honour of being the first to invent calculus.

In an exchange of letters with Newton's secretary, Samuel Clarke, Leibniz sets out his view on the matter of Indiscernibles. Indiscernibles are very small things, of course. But it was, nonetheless, an issue with Implications – not only for Newton's conviction that he had found 'Absolute Space' in his bucket (experiment N), but also in the question of which of the two deserved the greater share of the honour for the discovery of the powerful new mathematics. These vexed questions were pursued in an exchange of letters. We join Leibniz at his fourth attempt to settle the matter.

> There is no such thing as two individuals indiscernible from each other. An ingenious gentleman of my acquaintance, discoursing with me, in the presence of Her Electoral Highness the Princess Sophia [Newton, of such humble origins, grinds his teeth here], in the garden of Herrenhausen; thought he could find two leaves perfectly alike. The Princess defied him to do it, and he ran all over the garden for a long time to look for some; but it was to no purpose. Two drops of water, or milk, viewed with a microscope, will appear distinguishable from each other. This is an argument against atoms; which are confuted, as well as a vacuum, by the principles of true metaphysics . . .

The Identity of Indiscernibles

To suppose two things indiscernible, is to suppose [as Newton's Mr Clarke had just done] the same thing under two names. And therefore to suppose that the universe could have had at first another position of time and place, than that which it actually had; and yet that all the parts of the universe should have had the same situation among themselves, as that which they actually had; such a supposition, I say, is an impossible fiction. . . . [Indeed] all empty space is an imaginary thing . . . if that space be empty, it will be an attribute without a subject, an extension without any thing extended. . . . If space is an a absolute reality . . . it will have a greater reality than substances themselves.* God cannot destroy it, nor even change it in any respect. It will be not only immense in the whole, but also immutable and eternal in every part. There will be an infinite number of eternal things besides God. . . .

It certainly sounds ridiculous. But what is wrong with imagining a universe in which 'all the parts' have the same relation to each other as they ever had, but which has nonetheless been moved, has 'another position of time and place'?

Surely (not that poor Mr Clarke is able to come up with one at the time), a 'mirror image universe', one simply flipped over, would have these indiscernible characteristics yet still be very – discernibly – different?

* As Kant thought, see experiment K.

Discussion

Leibniz worried that if you had two individuals that had the same appearance and the same memories, personality and so on, then they would not only be impossible to tell apart (in the manner of naughty identical twins), but – by his principle of the identity of indiscernibles – they would in fact be the same person or 'thing'. This was unavoidable for Leibniz as he had already decided that spatial distinctions were illusory and so could not be used to distinguish one thing from another, which might sound odd, but then we do sometimes accept that approach with relation to time and place. For example, the flower in the garden yesterday is still the same flower even if it is today in a vase indoors.

Wittgenstein too would later ask us to imagine a world in which all human beings look exactly alike, so that it appears as if certain characteristics migrate amongst identical bodies. 'Under such circumstances, although it would be possible to give bodies names, we should perhaps be as little inclined to do so as we are to give names to the chairs of our dining room. On the other hand it might be useful to give names to the sets of characteristics. . . .'

In modern day Quantum mechanics, subatomic particles may share all the same characteristics, and spatial location can be the only way to tell one from another – yet spatial location for a subatomic particle is a matter for conjecture and surmise. For that reason, Quantum mechanics, like Leibniz, says that if two things cannot, even in principle, be distinguished, then they are the same thing. (For example, if a particle flickered in and out of existence, it would be the same particle, not one disappearing and being 'replaced' by an identical one.) In the mind-transfer/body-exchange machine, 'place' is not important either. We do not dispute the possibility (imaginary though it is) of a person being as it were instantaneously projected to a different location and yet still being the 'same person'. Even if they are now made up of different atoms and so on, or even if some large part of 'them' has been changed – tweedy Gibb for sporty Steve, for example.

The idea, in the *Upanishads*, that we could wake up in a changed location, with a different body and a different mind, having lost our memories of our old existence, is used by *Vedānta* to conclude that it is only the Self (*Atman*) that has real independent existence, and physical objects are illusions. It may sound implausible to a hard-headed materialist, but in a sense, we wake up in a different body every morning, with a different mind and with different (increasingly hazy) memories. So Buddhism adopts a kind of equally hard-headed empiricism where nothing really exists, not mind, nor matter, nor space and time themselves. All that is left in Buddhism is the notion of 'the moment'.

By contrast, Messers Newton and Clarke want to make not only matter and time 'real', but space too. (Without 'absolute space' their theories of mechanics would just fall apart.) Only mind seems to be left out, an anachronism in an increasingly mechanical world, even if Newton himself searched lifelong through the alchemical works of the ancients for just such a unifying element. Mr Leibniz accepts that matter and time exist, but is not so sure about 'space'. Instead, he ties the whole thing up with the mind of God.

From Leibniz's fifth letter to Samuel Clarke

> To conclude. If the space (which the author fancies) void of all bodies, is not altogether empty; what is it then full of? Is it full of extended spirits perhaps, of material substances, capable of extending and contracting themselves; which hover therein and penetrate each other without inconveniency, as the shadows of two bodies penetrate one another upon the surface of a wall... Nay, some have fancies that man, in the state of innocency, had also the gift of [ahem...] penetration; and that he became solid, opaque, and impenetrable by his fall. Is it not overthrowing our notions of things, to make God have parts, to make spirits have extension? The principle of the want of a sufficient reason does alone drive away these spectres of the imagination. Men easily run into fictions, for want of making a right use of that great principle...
>
> I don't say that matter and space are the same thing. I only say, there is no space where there is no matter; and that space in itself is not an absolute reality. Space and matter differ, as time and motion. However, these things, though different, are inseparable.

J is for Henri Poincaré and Alternative Geometries*

SPECIAL EQUIPMENT NEEDED: **highly extendable ladder**

Imagine a planet made only of gases. At the centre the temperature is very high, and this is where all the gaseous people evolved and normally live. At the surface, however, the temperature is very, very low. In fact, M. Poincaré tells us, it is absolute zero. (The significance of this will become clear later.)

As the gaseous people, let us call them 'the Jeometers', move around their planet, a small but subtle change takes place. Because of the change in temperature, the further they go from the centre, the smaller they become. And not just them, the smaller all the creatures and all the artefacts of the gaseous planet become. The most import-ant thing is that everything changes at exactly the same rate, so nothing gets out of kilter.

One year, the Jeometers determine they must explore the upper reaches of their planet and construct a massive ladder which they stand upright with its top disappearing far into the clouds. One of the Jeometers' geometers sets off up it, with the task of finding out how far the gaseous planet extends. There is great excitement, but it is dissipated somewhat when the geometer returns a few days later to say the ladder is nowhere near long enough.

For years and years sections of ladder are added, but it seems it is in vain. Each time the geometers return to say that the ladder is still not long enough.

Actually, as they ascend the ladder, both the Jeometers and the ladder itself are shrinking, shrinking so small that it is physically

---

* 'J' is for 'Jules', Henri Poncaré's real first name that he didn't like much. It is of course not acceptable as an alternative way of spelling jeometry.

Figure 5 Poincaré's ladder

impossible for them to ever get to the outer surface. (At absolute zero, they will shrink to absolutely nothing.) Yet as they climb up, becoming colder and colder and at the same time smaller and smaller, the steps on the ladder, their measuring rods – everything – are also getting smaller and smaller, so they never realize the shrinking is happening. Eventually, the Jeometers decide their planet is infinitely large. Which it isn't.

The problem is, whose measurements are the 'real ones'?

Discussion

M. Poincaré takes up the story:

> A moving object will become smaller and smaller as it approaches the circumference of the sphere. Let us observe, in the first place, that although from the point of view of our geometers this world is finite, to its inhabitants it will appear infinite.

Henri's point is a simple one. Nothing in the story is against the rules of logic, however unlikely given our everyday experiences of nature. Yet it appears to show that the assumptions of the truths of geometry, indeed the laws of the universe, are not beyond doubt. The gaseous people say that their planet is infinite, and as they can never step outside it, for them it is. Yet from the perspective of any passing space traveller, they are living an illusion.

The Ancient Greek geometers left a legacy of respect for the eternal truths of their science, and the certainty of their truths. Yet do the angles of a triangle always add up to 180°? Is it really certain that parallel lines never meet? Only if we assume that space is 'flat'.

Henri Poincaré's answer to Jeometers and geometers alike is the same: no measurements can be said to be the 'real ones' – it is all just a matter of convention.

K is for the *Kritik* and Kant's Kind of Thought Experiments

SPECIAL EQUIPMENT NEEDED: **strong brew, several volumes of Kant's writings**

In the *Critique of Pure Reason* (that is, of course, the *Kritik der reinen Vernunft*), Kant offers a new way of thinking about the world, what he calls speculative reason. Speculative reason can make space for extending our knowledge, even if it has to leave that space empty, awaiting the mundane work of practical reason to fill it later. For speculative reason, like thought experiments, can:

* survey its own power to choose the different ways in which objects are thought;
* provide a complete list of the varied ways in which it can pose problems for itself.

Neither experimental science, nor yet the rules of logic can do this. For, as he puts it in the Preface:

> reason should not learn from nature like a schoolchild, who merely regurgitates whatever the teacher wants, but like an authoritative judge, who compels the witnesses to answer the questions he asks them.

Indeed, Kant says his humble book can be taken as a kind of 'thought experiment'. So let's (briefly) try one of Kant's experiments, buried about half way through the *Kritik*. It is one of his four famous antinomies. Although ostensibly concerned with space and time, these shed very little light (like the rest of his magisterial works) on practical matters, but are rather concerned with the nature of thought itself.

In this, the second antinomy, Kant investigates the question of whether the universe is made up of little atomic bits, or whether in fact there is only an unending myriad of different substances and entities. He reasons that on the one hand, if there were no simple building blocks, then there could be no complex structures either. But if there were no building blocks and no complex structures then ... there would be nothing left to exist. But something does exist! So ... it seems that there must be some simple, atomic substances.

On the other hand, any such building block must take up some space. In fact, anything that can be observed from outside in one sense acquires what he calls the 'property of composition'. But in that case, can space also be broken down into small parts? Clearly not. Space does not consist of little bits or parts, but just of space. In which case:

> The absolutely simple is a mere idea, the objective reality of which cannot be demonstrated in any possible experience ... as the absolutely simple object cannot be given in any experience, and the world of sense must be considered the sum total of all possible experiences: nothing simple exists in the world.

It's a different kind of thought experiment, certainly.

The question is, as Kant puts it:

'whether there exists anywhere, or perhaps, in my own thinking Self, an indivisible and indestructible unity – or whether nothing but what is divisible and transitory exists'?

Discussion

Philosophers celebrate the simplicity and 'elegance' of the four antinomies, a compliment which has to be understood in the context of the rest of the book.

Immanuel Kant was one of a new breed of academic philosophers, with salaries that at last enabled them to churn out long learned accounts of things even if no one really cared about them anyway (although to be fair to his predecessors, they'd not done too badly before). Over his long and distinguished career he dealt with the difference between the *a priori* and the *a posteriori*, as well as the relation of the synthetic and the analytic. He even combines these studies to distinguish between the synthetic *a priori* (such as the axioms of geometry) and the analytic *a priori*, or maybe even the analytic *a posteriori* which he didn't seem to think existed anyway. All this in between apparently dining out every lunch and evening with scholarly friends and hosting the beloved 'card parties'. Not to mention managing to invent the Transcendental Aesthetic and the Cosmological Idea of Freedom, and the Cosmical Conception – nor to forget the famous Categorical Imperative.

Alas, as the poor translator for the original English edition of Kant's great work, wrote in a special apologetic preface:

> He [Kant] had never studied the art of expression. He wearies by frequent repetitions, and employs a great number of words to express, in the clumsiest way, what could have been enounced more clearly and distinctly in a few.

But clumsy though his writing may be, Kant is more famous for his thinking. And thought experiments – the *ens imaginarium* or even the *nihil privativum*, (the empty intuition that relates to no real experience, or the imagining of something that does not 'in reality' exist, as Kant bafflingly would like us to classify them) – are a big part of that.

As we've seen, buried in the heart of what the translator calls 'the maze' are the 'Four Antinomies', designed (like Zeno's paradoxes) to show the limits of 'reason'. Kant introduces them confidently thus:

> These dialectical propositions are so many attempts to solve four natural and unavoidable problems of reason. There are neither more, nor can there be less, than there are this number, because there are no other series of synthetical hypotheses, limiting *a priori* the empirical synthesis.

Kant continues:

The questions: whether the world has a beginning and a limit to its extension in space; whether there exists anywhere, or perhaps, in my own thinking Self, an indivisible and indestructible unity – or whether nothing but what is divisible and transitory exists [*that was our one by the way*]; whether I am a free agent, or, like other beings, am bound in the chains of nature and fate; whether, finally, there is a supreme cause of the world, or all our thought and speculation must end with nature and the order of external things – are questions for the solution of which the mathematician would willingly exchange his whole science; for in it there is no satisfaction for the highest aspirations and most ardent desires of humanity. Nay, it may even be said that the true value of mathematics – that pride of human reason – consists in this: that she guides reason to the knowledge of nature, in her greater as well as in her less manifestations, in her beautiful order and regularity – guides her, moreover, to an insight into the wonderful unity of the moving forces in the operations of nature, far beyond the expectations of a philosophy building only on experience; and that she thus encourages philosophy to extend the province of reason beyond all experience, and at the same time provides it with the most excellent materials for supporting its investigations, in so far as their nature admits, by adequate and accordant intuitions.

So, is everything divisible – or not?

Unfortunately for speculation – but perhaps fortunately for the practical interests of humanity – reason, in the midst of her highest anticipations, finds herself hemmed in by a press of opposite and contradictory conclusions, from which neither her honour nor her safety will permit her to draw back. Nor can she regard these conflicting trains of reasoning with indifference as mere passages at arms, still less can she command peace; for in the subject of the conflict she has a deep interest. There is no other course left open to her than to reflect with herself upon the origin of this disunion in reason – whether it may not arise from a mere misunderstanding. After such an inquiry, arrogant claims would have to be given up on both sides; but the sovereignty of reason over understanding and sense would be based upon a sure foundation.

It is not, to be sure, a very clear answer, but perhaps what Mr Kant is saying is that there is a place and indeed a role for the thought experiment technique, even in such thorny metaphysical issues.

L is for Lucretius' Spear

SPECIAL EQUIPMENT NEEDED: **spear**

Lucretius' Spear is one of the most ancient and yet most fruitful thought experiments. It raises fundamental questions not only for astronomers but also for physicists about the nature of the universe and of infinity.

Lucretius' spear is a real wood and metal one, which in an epic poem he describes carrying to (and this is the difficult part) the very edge of the universe. Then, with a great roar and a big hurl, he tosses it over the boundary and into the infinity beyond.

What do you suppose happens next? Lucretius asks. And there are only two possibilities. Either the spear crosses the boundary and carries on (even if it then disappears), in which case the boundary is not truly the edge of the universe at all . . . or the spear cannot cross, but bounces off some sort of invisible force field or the like, in which case the line we thought was the edge of the universe is not the true boundary at all, but merely inside it, and the spear has yet to cross it.

And what if the wall at the edge of the universe itself is infinitely wide?

Discussion

Suppose for a moment that the whole of space *were* bounded and that someone made their way to its uttermost boundary and threw a flying spear. Do you suppose that the missile, hurled with might and main, would speed along the course on which it was aimed? Or do you think something would block the way and stop it? You must assume one alternative or the other. But neither of them leaves you so much as a loophole to wriggle through. Both force you to admit that the universe continues without end. Whether there is some obstacle lying on the boundary line that prevents the spear from going farther on its course, or whether it flies on beyond, it cannot in fact have started from the boundary. (Book I, 'Matter and Space', in *De Rerum Natura*)

De Rerum Natura, 'On the Nature of Things', is an unusual book, let alone poem. Written at some point in the hundred years preceding the first millennium, Lucretius describes his poem as a 'honey-coated' pill containing some unpalatable truths about the universe. Truths discovered by the great philosopher Epicurus, such as that everything in the universe is made up of just two things: empty space and tiny, invisible particles. That these particles can neither be created, nor destroyed. And (as this experiment is intended to demonstrate) that the universe is infinite and contains all possible things and all possible worlds.

In fact, the view set out in the poem was far and away the best description of the universe at least up to the twentieth century, and for all our sophisticated models nowadays, maybe it remains in some ways superior to present thinking. For example, Lucretius, or rather Epicurus, specifically added a little 'swerve' to the movement of the particles, so as to allow for the possibility of free will in our human lives. Otherwise, the universe and everything in it was no more meaningful than the ceaseless playing of the tiny motes in a sunbeam.

1,700 years of science later, it was still important to prove that the universe was infinite and unbounded. René Descartes and Isaac Newton both offered arguments to demonstrate this, concerned that otherwise Aristotle's view of a finite universe seemed to limit God and to take the soul out of the machine. Yet in fact, as Einstein later pointed out, the universe can quite easily be both finite and unbounded – an anti-commonsensical view which might cause our spear carrier to stumble in confusion. But then, as Einstein also said (quite irrespective of whatever Kant might have liked), space does not *have to* obey the rules of geometry.

These days, in any case, cosmologists think that space may be mostly made up of invisible energy fields with what we used to think of as 'the universe' simply floating in it, suspended, as it were, in a dark soup of anti-gravity.

But what's the soup in?

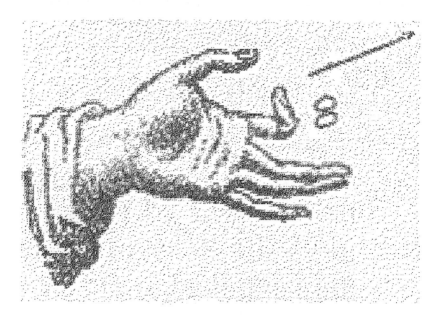

Figure 6 Lucretius' spear

M is for Mach's Motionless Chain

SPECIAL EQUIPMENT NEEDED: **funny shaped block of ice, cannon balls, wire**

Ernst Mach is credited with coining the term 'thought experiment', or to be more precise, *Gedankenexperiment*, and was himself a keen experimenter. In *The Science of Mechanics* (1893) he set out his view that people all possess a deep reservoir of 'instinctive knowledge' which we can both add to and draw on without being consciously aware of it.

His favourite example was the rather unlikely (technical) scenario of a chain draped around a frictionless right-angled triangle.* However, we can do slightly better than this. I have changed the chain for the more exciting case of a series of cannon balls joined by wire, the whole lot carefully laid on a block of (still almost frictionless) ice so that the ends are at the same height. And in a final bit of melomach-drama, we imagine the experimenter under one end of the chain of cannon balls, waiting to see if the theory was correct.

The lurking doubt for Ernst, as he sweats there, is whether the steeper slope of the ice above him will prove a greater influence on the matter than the clearly superior number of cannon balls on the far side.

How can Ernst be sure he is safe?

---

* Following up on the medieval philosopher, Stevin, who had discussed a similar problem to investigate the question of the weight required to balance another weight on an inclined plane.

Figure 7a Mach worried about motions

Discussion

He imagines that before risking his hat he had added a few links to the chain and gently allowed the whole system to settle. Now several things become obvious.

What is obvious? That we can remove the section of 'cannon balls on wire' under the horizontal, as they cannot disturb the balls above. In both this and our original set-up neither side of the chain can start to move, for if it were to do so, we would have created a perpetual motion machine – worse than that, a perpetual motion generating engine – and that, although desirable in a sense, would offend against the laws of physics, and what's more, common sense. But now, and here's the clever bit, having dispensed with all the balls below the base of the triangle, it is also obvious that there is not only a relationship between the number of balls on one side and on the other, but, more usefully, that the weights are in the same relationship as the lengths of the sides.

Mach commented in *The Science of Mechanics*,

we accept the conclusion drawn . . . without the thought of an objection, although the law if presented as the simple result of experiment . . . would appear dubious.

And our gallant armchair experimenter is safe and sound too.

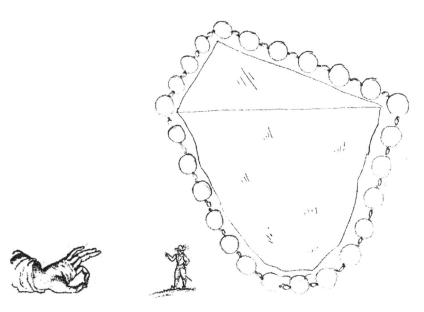

Figure 7b   Mach mightily reassured

N is for Newton's Bucket

SPECIAL EQUIPMENT NEEDED: **a bucket and a long piece of rope**

Presenting the experiment to the Royal Society, Sir Isaac Newton. *In which*, Sir Isaac will argue for Absolute Space and Absolute Motion using a bucket and a long piece of rope.

To start with, Newton's imaginary assistant fills the bucket with water and then suspends it on the long piece of rope from a rafter. The bucket is then turned round and round until the rope is fully twisted.

The assistant reminds us that when you stir tea in a cup, it eventually swirls round and round until it assumes a concave shape, slightly higher at the sides of the cup than at the middle. (But this could be due to friction between the tea and the stationary 'wall' of the cup, someone mutters. Or something.)

Now, Newton says, 'release the bucket!' and his assistant does. It twists round and round wonderfully smoothly as the long rope unwinds. At first, of course, the water in the bucket is level. When the circular motion starts, the water gradually becomes higher at the edges and lower at the middle, as the water 'climbs up' the rotating walls of the bucket, in this sense, a bit like the tea in the cup.

'For a short while, though, the bucket was in relative motion to the water' shouts Newton enthusiastically to the audience, 'but was level!'

Eventually however, the water 'catches up' with the bucket, and both are soon whirling round, in a circular sort of way, at the same speed. Any friction between the two disappears. And yet, as Newton proudly points out, despite this, the concave shape of the water in the bucket persists.

SUDDENLY NEWTON'S ASSISTANT STEPS IN AND GRABS THE WHIRLING BUCKET AND STOPS ITS MOTION!

The water continues whirling around inside it for a few moments. And it continues to have its 'concave' shape, and is in the same sort of relative motion to the bucket as it was at the beginning of the experiment. Although it was flat then.

Relative to each other, the water and the bucket are both moving, but only in one case is the water a concave shape, explains Newton. 'Is the motion different relative to the building, the floor, the Earth?' asks a member of the audience helpfully. 'Not at all', says Sir Isaac, 'the water is showing the effects of centrifugal force, and galaxies themselves are affected by centrifugal forces. The only thing that it is relative to', Newton pauses here for effect, 'is Absolute Space itself'.

Has the water in Newton's bucket detected the existence of Absolute Space, as he claims?

Discussion

In part VII of his *Principia*, Newton writes:

> Absolute Space, in its own nature, without relation to anything external, remains always similar and immovable.

In fact, Newton thought that even if everything material in the universe were to disappear, Absolute Space would remain. It would be empty, but still a real 'space'. Time would remain too.

The bucket experiment is supposed to show simply that the shape of the water does not depend on its relative motion to the sides of the bucket. Interestingly, in the original *Principia*, Newton describes only the first half of our experiment. In later accounts the bucket is stopped by an 'assistant' and no one knows quite who suggested it – or why – any more. But perhaps himself already wondering whether his bucket experiment alone was enough to carry conviction, Newton does also ask us to imagine two globes tied together and whirled around their centre of gravity. The two globes will both try to fly off at a tangent, but, being restrained by the cord between them, will instead put the cord under tension.

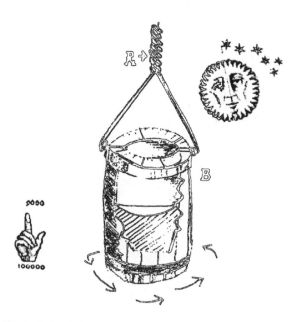

Figure 8   Newton's bucket

On the other hand, if all motion is relative, then there should be no difference between stationary observation of rotating globes, and rotating observation of stationary globes. Say, by sitting in the bucket with two globes on the floor beneath and a cord stretched between them. *Now as the observer whirls around it could appear to them that the globes were being whirled instead. But a glance at the cord on the ground would reveal that it was not under any tension.

Later on, Ernst Mach would say the universe is influencing every-thing all the time, and that Newton was wrong to imagine everything away. 'Try to fix Newton's bucket in place and rotate the heavenly firmament and then prove the absence of centrifugal forces instead', he scoffs. Nor should anyone assume that they know what would happen if there was 'rotating observation of the globes' in a universe with everything else removed. (Imagine that!)

---

* There is no evidence that Newton actually tried this.

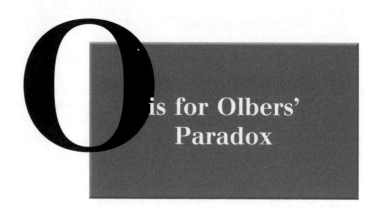

is for Olbers' Paradox

Olbers thought that, given that the universe is so vast and there are so many stars in it (and assuming the stars are not all clumped in one corner), when we look at the night sky we should see stars everywhere we look. In fact, the night sky should be so brightly lit up that it should look as though completely filled from side to side by one giant star. The paradox is . . . that it doesn't.

Actually, the paradox, although technical, touches upon profound issues in cosmology, or the study and theory of the origins of the universe. Simply saying that most of the stars are too far away to see is not enough. Certainly it is true that starlight, like any other kind of light, dims as a function of distance, but at the same time, the number of light sources in the 'cone of vision' increases – at exactly the same rate.* In fact, on the mathematics of it, given an infinite universe, with galaxies and stars distributed uniformly, the whole night sky should appear to be not black, not speckled, but white.

Heinrich Olbers (1758–1840) was a Viennese doctor who only did astronomy in his spare time, and although the paradox carries his name, it can really be traced back to Johannes Kepler in 1610. (Kepler is remembered instead for his work on the orbits of planets around the sun.) Olbers' contribution (apart from some maths) was to realize that the problem was even greater than Kepler had thought. If the universe was infinite in size, as everyone was saying, the night sky would not only be bright – but *infinitely bright.*

So why isn't it?

---

* Decreasing at $1/r^2$ and increasing at r^2.

Discussion

Olbers' paradox is a 'thought experiment' in the very good sense that most of the reasoning is done by hypotheticals. What if the universe is infinitely large? And infinitely old? If the stars and galaxies are (on average) spread out evenly? Similarly, the search for solutions is also – of necessity – done in the 'laboratory of the mind'.

And people have concocted various possible explanations. Such as:

- Perhaps there's too much dust in space to see the distant stars;
- or the universe has only a finite number of stars and galaxies;
- or maybe the stars and galaxies are not – even 'on average' – distributed randomly, but rather clumped together leaving most of space completely empty. So, for example, there could be a lot of stars, but they hide behind one another.

The first idea is tempting, but ignores known facts. Like that the dust would heat up too, and that space would have a much higher

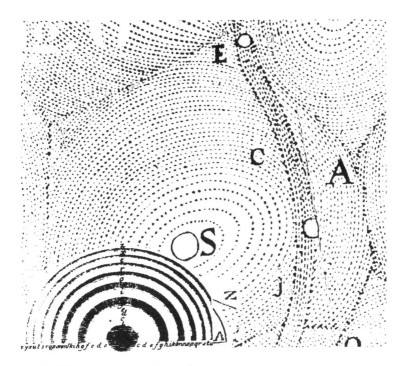

Figure 9   Olbers' astronomical paradox

temperature than it does. And that it would require a lot of dust to block out the light – so much in fact that we should find it also blocking the light from the sun. Since we don't find either happening, the future for this explanation looks (ahem) a bit dim . . .

On the other hand, the second suggestion could well be correct. But the number of stars, finite or not, is definitely still large enough to light up the entire sky. The explanation only saves us from being 'fried'.

So in the nineteenth century the preferred 'solution' was the third option. That although infinite, the heavens were erratically populated, allowing large areas of the night sky to appear empty. But this was a little opportunistic, and in any case observations today show that the uniformity assumption is not so very far off the mark. Telescopes orbiting the earth have confirmed that the universe is effectively a smooth, thin gruel, for all the local irregularities we may live and die on.

So what is the answer to Olbers' question? The favoured explanation today is that although the universe may be infinitely large, it is perhaps not infinitely old, meaning that the galaxies beyond a certain distance will simply not have had enough time to send their light over to fill our night sky. If the universe is, say, 15 billion years old, then only stars and galaxies less than 15 billion light years away are going to be visible.

Sometimes added to this (in the manner of all dodgy explanations) is the new theory that if the universe is expanding all the time (after the so-called 'big bang'), some galaxies may be travelling so fast 'away from us' that their light has become dimmed by 'red shift', the phenomenon which sort of stretches out a star's wavelength beyond the visible spectrum.

Thus, in making a few imaginary assumptions and asking his seemingly simple question, 'Why is the night sky dark?' Olbers and the others created a thought experiment that actually pointed to two of the great 'discoveries' of modern astronomy: namely that the universe seems to be expanding and is almost certainly of only a very finite age.

P is for Parfit's Person

SPECIAL EQUIPMENT NEEDED: **an unscrupulous brain surgeon**

For our tweedy academic of scenario B, or even the conscientious cannibal of scenario C, the 'preservation of essential matter' is a key concern. It is also a concern of Derek Parfit's. But being a philosopher, he thinks it is all much more straightforward. As long as your brain is preserved. (Say by a brain transplant to another body.)

The main consideration for him is to what extent his 'mental' attributes, along with his brain, are being transferred. Clearly one expects these to include one's 'character' (soul) in some sense. Provided the brain carried with it your memories, your personal 'psychological' traits and characteristics, the resulting person would seem to still be you, and this would provide a method (albeit rather an unethical one) for rejuvenation.

Of course, such an operation would be tricky. But worse problems arise, Derek thinks, when parts of your brain are put into different people. For example, what would happen if it turned out that half a brain was enough to do the trick? So much the better, some might assume, half left in case something goes wrong the first time. But what, Derek Parfit asks, if the other half of your brain is transplanted into another body with equal success. Wouldn't there then be two of you? A sort of mental cloning?

Yet how could there be two people 'identical' with your former self? How would anyone know who to invite to parties?

Indeed, how would you know which one was really you?

Discussion

Some philosophers say that the two new people would not be identical with each other, because they would be in different places having different experiences at the same time. In fact, as time went on, they would diverge more and more from each other. Yet it would still appear rather arbitrary, given their equal claims, to say that the first person receiving the new brain one was the 'new you', and the other one not. (See . . . er . . . experiment I.)

Perhaps better to say that neither of them is really you. But in that case, you have now perished, even though, before the second transplant, it seemed that you were happily continuing in a nice new youthful body. Funnily enough, if the second transplant had failed, it seems 'you' would still be happily continuing in your new body. After all, the second operation was performed on someone else and 'you' need not even have known about it. But this in itself raises odd questions. How could it be that what is done to one person should result in another ceasing to exist?

At this point, Derek Parfit says that such dependence on what happens to someone else is impossible and concludes it is better to suppose that even the recipient of the 'whole' brain transplant should not have been thought of as really being 'you'. In which case, your identity ceased at the time of the first transplant.

But do not be too sad. Parfit's considered opinion is that we do not need to cling too much to our personhood. Something of us would survive in the transplanting – but not the Thing that was us before. Not, in his term, our 'identity'.

Some say this is not a very strong sense of 'survive'. One contemporary philosopher, Kelly Ross, says it is only like the sense in which one might be said to 'survive' in one's heirs, or through those who carry on one's life work. But Parfit would be quite happy at the survival being only in a weak sense. For he imagines, like the Buddhists, that we would be less anxious for 'ourselves', and less selfish towards 'others', if only we realized that the idea of a continuing self is an illusion. He warns those who believe in a continuing self, that they are continuing to be misled by René Descartes' theory: the one that says we have an immaterial ego. (Located in the pineal gland, brain surgeons please note.)

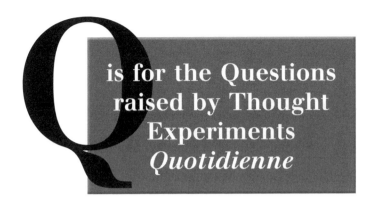

Q is for the Questions raised by Thought Experiments
Quotidienne

SPECIAL EQUIPMENT NEEDED: clock

Quotidienne being 'everyday' and the term given by the contemporary French philosopher, Roger-Pol Droit, to a series of mental gymnastics designed to broaden the mind and make it more supple. Some of the exercises seem really rather silly, such as ringing up telephone numbers at random (this to make yourself feel insignificant), and pinching yourself hard (this to acquaint yourself with the reality of pain). But others are really rather thoughtful. Take two experiments to do with the nature of space and time. The first is the Twenty-Minute World thought experiment.

Imagine the world only lasts 20 minutes. That is, imagine it sprang into existence just a moment ago, and will pop out of existence too in just exactly 20 minutes. Everything in the world appeared exactly as it now is, out of the flux. 'Like a soap-bubble bursting, or a light going out', it will disappear in 19 minutes.

Roger-Pol Droit says that (doing this) everything looks the same, yet something has changed. The world lacks the depth of 'a real past and the perspective of a viable future'. And as the 20 minutes approaches its term, we should feel 'furtively, the dumb terror that everything will, effectively, disappear'. Although, as Roger-Pol drolly remarks, perhaps secretly we will also feel a slight disappointment if nothing is obliterated . . .

But another *Expérience Quotidienne* is (for me anyway) perhaps more subtle. It involves finding a landscape or view to sit down and contemplate. Then the experiment starts.

You settle down to look at it. Don't stare. Don't scrutinize. There's nothing for your eye to seek out, and it should avoid stopping at any

67

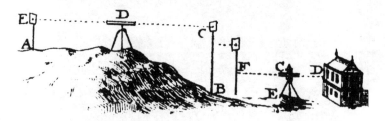

Figure 10 Tweeking the curtain . . .

particular point. On the contrary, let it glide over the whole, disengaged and slightly vague . . . everything must seem to you like a single surface, flat and without relief – like a painting.

This may take a few minutes to achieve, although Roger-Pol says it can happen very fast depending on your mood. Anyway, when you really believe you are staring at a single smooth surface, then imagine that 'everything you see, from earth to sky, whether still or in motion, is just a detail on an immense, stretched canvas.' Or perhaps on a giant screen, 'like a gigantic cinema screen, shown in perfect focus and definition'. And now imagine the screen is being folded up.

You are about to see this great curtain, which contains the entire landscape, reveal something behind itself, as, very slowly, it starts to fold.

What will you see, asks Roger-Pol?

Discussion

And in this latter experiment, Roger-Pol Droit says we can imagine anything we like, but one thing we should see is that, from now on, 'the solidity of the real' has been diminished.

These '*expériences quotidiennes*' are not really thought experiments at all,* in the same sense as the other ones favoured by our scientists and analytic philosophers. They are neither logically compelling, nor are they pretending to be. This, after all, is French philosophy, and at a certain point the Continental and English-speaking ('Anglo-American') philosophers parted company. Nonetheless, I think the same technique is there. And, in a way, the 'evidence' of such musings is no more to be dismissed than the evidence of more conventional thought – or even practical – experiments.

---

* Certainly the two 'silly' ones aren't, involving actual physical action.

R is for the Rule-Ruled Room

SPECIAL EQUIPMENT NEEDED: **pile of Chinese hieroglyphs**

Alan Turing it was, the celebrated Second World War code-breaker, who suggested that when we are unable to tell the difference, after prolonged questioning, between talking to a machine or to a human being, we ought to consider the machine to have intelligence.

This offended many philosophers. After all, intelligence is something hard acquired and jealously guarded. And it was in the celebrated 'Chinese Room' experiment that philosophers found their champion. It was there, that the (contemporary) artificially intelligent philosopher, John Searle, sought to debunk such a generous interpretation.

Searle offers to be locked up in the imaginary room with a pile of Chinese hieroglyphs. He then asks us to consider what would appear to happen if, from time to time, someone outside the room were to post Chinese questions through the letter box for him to sort out. Now, as it happens, inside the room there are some instructions taped on the wall, written in English, which explain precisely which hieroglyph to post back, no matter which one is posted in.

Searle's aim is to prove that such a person in such a room does not understand Chinese. Since computers operate in an analogous way, he then goes on to say that it's not really accurate to say that computers are intelligent or understand things, even if they produce intelligent-looking responses.

The experiment is fairly convincing at showing that the person in the room does not understand Chinese. After all, at the beginning of his example, he states that they 'know no Chinese, either written or spoken', and that for them, 'Chinese writing is just so many meaningless squiggles.' His conclusion may seem a bit like stating the obvious but, well, analytic philosophers do that sort of stuff. The trick is to make the obvious seem not so obvious. Nonetheless, the philosophical problem remains as Searle puts it, that 'from the external point of view – that is, from the point of view of somebody outside the room in which I am locked – my answers to the questions are absolutely indistinguishable from those of native Chinese speakers.'

So, does the experiment show that intelligence is more than just appearances?

Discussion

But what Professor Searle *seems* to have missed is that it is not so much that the person in the room appears to understand Chinese, but that the whole 'system' – person in the room, sets of symbols on cards, plus instructions taped to the wall – gives the appearance of understanding Chinese. And this is much more plausible. After all, whoever wrote the instructions did understand Chinese.

What has happened in his example is that the expertise of the instructions' author has been transferred, via the written rules, to the person in the room. If the set-up is then replaced by a computer, programmed with the rules, then the 'expertise' of the Chinese speaker has, at least in limited cases, been transferred to the computer. This approach makes it much more difficult for Searle, or anyone else, to deny the computer any expertise or even understanding. And actually, these days, you may be treated in hospitals, given career advice, told where to dig for gold, who to drop bombs on, or whatever, by computers running 'expert systems' of rules and procedures drawn from human expertise.

Broadening the issue of whether computers really think, Professor Wang of Qingdao University (who really does understand Chinese) says the question in any case, is not whether the machine demonstrates intelligence, but whether 'this human construct' demonstrates intelligence. Lisa Wang notes that a picture, after all, may be said to be 'of a tree', or 'beautiful', or whatever, even if it is basically just bits of mineral squashed onto a piece of vegetable.

The Chinese Room may be just another misguided attempt at understanding the world by reducing it to its parts – a congenital mistake often committed by analytical philosophers and quite contrary, of course, to the Eastern, indeed the Socratic tradition. (Although it is a bit like Aristotle's way.) As Leibniz put it, in the *Monadology*:

> Suppose that there were a machine so constructed as to produce thought, feeling, and perception. We could imagine it increased in size while retaining the same proportions, so that one could enter as one might a mill. On going inside we should only see the parts impinging upon one another, we should not see anything which would explain a perception . . .

But this is getting complicated. I should like to suggest another 'thought experiment' – my own humble version of this interesting problem. (Searle did several, getting increasingly complex and obscure.)

The Chinese Room Experiment (cruel version)

SPECIAL EQUIPMENT NEEDED: **pile of philosophy books**

Suppose a person is locked in a room stripped of furniture, apart from a typewriter and a table piled high with dusty old philosophy books. And then suppose on the wall is a blackboard with instructions on how to use them – especially on how to look up views on certain philosophical problems. Now, into this room are posted some tantalizing questions such as:

- Is 'the void' a normative concept?
- Do thought experiments offer access to a world of *a priori* truths?
- Can we look at something and imagine it – at exactly the same time?

and so on . . .

Then, using the instructions, our prisoner types out relevant sections from the philosophy books and posts them back. You see, our prisoner does not understand philosophy. They think it is all just meaningless squiggles.

But to anyone outside the room, the prisoner appears to understand.

So now does the experiment show that philosophy is more than just appearances? Remember Alan Turing says that to distinguish between the appearance and the actualité is mere prejudice – Searle is not so sure.

What I think is interesting about this experiment is that it seems to highlight that although we are reluctant to allow someone locked in the Chinese Room to be credited with 'understanding' a language just because they can reliably produce the correct response to questions, this is not really so obviously reasonable. As anyone who has been to philosophical seminars and similar discussions will know, it is not necessary – and certainly not appreciated – to generate your own view on the problems but better, rather, to appropriately reproduce other people's views and comments.

Why tell the philosopher who offers such second-hand contributions that they 'do not really' understand? Only a cad would do so, Prof. Searle!

Happily, at least as far as the so-called 'Cruel Room' example goes, there is another option available to researchers. And that is simply to wait and see if the occupant gets bored and tries to leave. In which case we can be pretty sure that they don't really understand philosophy.

S is for Salvatius' Ship, Sailing along its Own Space-Time Line

SPECIAL EQUIPMENT NEEDED: **a fish bowl and a convenient ferry service**

Salvatius explains the experiment this time.

Shut yourself up with some friend in the main cabin below decks on some large ship, and have with you there some flies, butterflies, and other small flying animals. Have a large bowl of water with some fish in it; hang up a bottle that empties drop by drop into a wide vessel beneath it.

With the ship standing still, observe carefully how the little animals fly with equal speed to all sides of the cabin. The fish swim indifferently in all directions; the drops fall into the vessel beneath; and, in throwing something to your friend, you need to throw it no more strongly in one direction than another, the distances being equal; jumping with your feet together, you pass equal spaces in every direction.

When you have observed all of these things carefully (though there is no doubt that when the ship is standing still everything must happen this way), have the ship proceed with any speed you like, so long as the motion is uniform and not fluctuating this way and that. You will discover not the least change in all the effects named, nor could you tell from any of them whether the ship was moving or standing still. In jumping, you will pass on the floor the same spaces as before, nor will you make larger jumps toward the stern than towards the prow even though the ship is moving quite rapidly, despite the fact that during the time that you are in the air the floor under you will be going in a direction opposite to your jump. In throwing something to your companion, you will need no more force to get it to him whether he is in the direction of the bow or the stern, with yourself situated opposite.

The droplets will fall as before into the vessel beneath without dropping towards the stern, although while the drops are in the air the ship

74

runs many spans. The fish in the water will swim towards the front of their bowl with no more effort than toward the back, and will go with equal ease to bait placed anywhere around the edges of the bowl. Finally the butterflies and flies will continue their flights indifferently toward every side, nor will it ever happen that they are concentrated toward the stern, as if tired out from keeping up with the course of the ship, from which they will have been separated during long intervals by keeping themselves in the air. . . .

SAGREDUS: Although it did not occur to me to put these observations to the test when I was voyaging, I am sure that they would take place in the way you describe. Indeed, I remember having often found myself in my cabin wondering whether the ship was moving or standing still; and sometimes at a whim, I have supposed it going one way when its motion was the opposite. . . . (Galileo, *Dialogues Concerning the Two Chief World Systems*, 1632)

But just what are Salvatius' little fish supposed to prove?

Discussion

The aim of Galileo's ship experiment, set out in his *Dialogues Concerning the Two Chief World Systems*, was to explain why, if the world really is a sphere whizzing round on its axis in space, we are unaware of it. Back in 1632, the idea that we lived on rock hurtling around the sun was still rather hard to swallow, and the now commonplace experience of smooth constant motion in one direction (for example, on a train, if not so much in a car) was still something of a rarity.

And thanks to the Christian Church, the thought experiments of Ptolemy, the ancient astronomer, geographer, and mathematician, still held sway. Amongst various arguments designed to bolster the 'Ptolemaic system' and prove that the Earth really was set immovably in position at the centre of the universe, was the simple one that since all bodies fall towards the centre of the universe, the Earth must be fixed there, otherwise we would not see falling objects drop as they do, toward the centre of the Earth. Likewise, if the Earth rotated on its axis every day, a ball thrown vertically upward would not fall back to the same place, but slightly to one side.

But 'the ship' illustrates that 'uniform horizontal motion' has no effect on the outcome of 'localized' experiments, which include the commonplace experiments of everyday sense perception. Only by stepping outside the local framework can measurements be made. To detect the motion of the ship, for example, we would have to look through the porthole at the receding cliffs, or the sun. To see the motion of the Earth itself, we must look at the night sky and the movement of the stars. (Of course, the cliffs *might* be shrinking, or the stars rotating on crystal spheres . . .)

The thought experiment has been resurrected in various similar forms subsequently by other physicists to provide further useful intuitions about the nature of the universe. It threw light on deficiencies in another of Aristotle's faulty axioms, namely that of 'Absolute Rest', as well as undermining Newton's pet nostrum of 'Absolute Space'. A more fruitful notion, the Principle of Equivalence, was introduced to physics instead. Christian Huygens (1629–95) later used it to improve his theory concerning the 'collisions of bodies', and in his novel, *Sylvie and Bruno*, Lewis Carroll (no less) described the difficulty of having tea inside a falling house, thereby anticipating by some years the famous 'falling lift' thought experiment. It is there that Einstein developed the concepts of 'inertial co-ordinate systems' and 'relative motion' into the first full-blown theory of relativity. (The ship's cabin is an inertial co-ordinate system, either when 'standing still', or proceeding 'with any speed you like, so long as the motion is uniform', and provides points of reference.)

In 1907 Einstein realized that extending the same principles to a spaceship steadily accelerating would demonstrate in similar manner the impossibility of distinguishing between the push of constant acceleration and the pull of gravity, and hence arrived at the General Theory of Relativity.

All that from just watching fish!

T is for the Time-Travelling Twins

SPECIAL EQUIPMENT NEEDED: **a spaceship**

In one of his science fiction stories, H. G. Wells imagined a Victorian inventor who sits in a time machine set up in his sitting room watching in wonderment as the sun sets and rises again in rapid succession, then marvelling as the leaves fall from the trees in the garden and sprout again, before finally (with a belching of smoke and a juddering of relative motion) his time traveller arrives in the far distant future. Shaken, as they say, but not unduly stirred.

Unfortunately, that is impossible as far as the technologies of today allow. But the idea of time travel is not only an old one; it's also a perfectly serious one. The prevailing mathematical description of our physical world, Einstein's theory of relativity, contains within it the possibility of time travel – both into the future and into the past. It is allowed by the universe. Just rather hard to do in practice.

But not for thought experimenters. For such people, as for H. G. Wells, practicality is not a problem. It is enough to conceive the possibility.

One of the best known imaginings is that of the Time-travelling Twins. Twin Two is left at mission control in Beijing, the other is sent to visit Alpha Centauri, on a very fast spaceship accelerating close to the speed of light. The twins thus bear their separation phlegmatically, one waiting for the return of the other.

But when the rocket eventually returns and Twin Two gets out, after a mere 20 thrilling but very tiring years speeding through the cosmos, the other twin is nowhere to be seen. What is this! How unappreciative! The explanation, when it comes, is no comfort. Although only 20 years went by on the rocket ship, and Twin Two is indeed 'only' 20 years older, back on Earth much, much longer has gone by, and Twin One is now an old and white-haired veteran, who has to be wheeled very slowly up to the steps of the rocket ship to visit Twin Two.

This then is the 'twins paradox' that has so delighted exponents of relativity theory as a way of demonstrating the effects of close-to-light-speed travel. And physicists have fairly convincingly demonstrated the effect with atomic clocks and the like. (Indeed, such time shifts are now part and parcel of the practical management of satellites in 'low Earth' orbit.)

Not content, though, with the implausibility of that, we might suppose that Twin Two now regrets the decision to fly off to the nearest star, and steps straight into the space centre 'time travel booth' (invented while the spaceship was away). Setting the dial to 101 years earlier, Twin Two intends to return to the past and persuade Twin One to come with them on the trip. Whizz, whizz, whizz! (Stars and nights become dawns and sunsets in rapid succession, snows fall and recede, and the space centre itself disappears to become a field of flowers.) Twin Two descends from the machine, walks to the nearest road, and seeing a car approaching, steps out to flag it down. By a strange coincidence, the car is being driven by none other than the absent-minded professor who years later was credited with inventing the time machine Twin Two has just used.

Unfortunately, the professor, brainy though she undoubtedly is, drives rather less than attentively (thinking of higher things) and is so startled that she accidentally swerves straight off the road and into a tree, thereby departing this earthly world and never inventing anything much.

The puzzling question for Twin Two is, how could a time traveller be responsible for killing the person who sent them on their journey in the first place?

Discussion

Twin Two is most puzzled at this question, as Twin Two subscribes to the view that time travellers must be somehow barred from altering patterns of cause and effect, lest the very fabric of the universe be 'torn asunder'. However, as Twin One shrugs later when the two eventually catch up, the illogicality of it at most rules out certain direct and completely unambiguous contradictions, not time travel in general. Perhaps the professor had already left the germ of the time machine idea to another . . . ?

Anyway, Twin One thinks the lesson is not that they should both go to Alpha Centauri but that they should both stay at home. In which case they won't need a time machine at all. 'But I've *already* used it!' exclaims Twin Two exasperatedly. And then pauses. Because now they come to think of it . . . in a sense they haven't. . . .

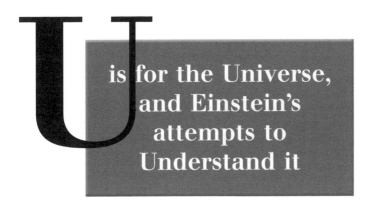

U is for the Universe, and Einstein's attempts to Understand it

SPECIAL EQUIPMENT NEEDED: **pier, waves**

When he was just a boy, Einstein liked to speculate on the nature of electromagnetic radiation. (It seems a bit odd, but there you are. More worryingly, he never grew out of it.) In particular, he wondered what would happen if you were able to run as fast as a ray of light.

To help him imagine this, he thought of running down a pier, from the seaward end, just as a big wave, say made by a speedboat swishing past, was approaching the shore. Now, if he ran at exactly the same speed, he realized, the watery wave would to him look like a stationary hump in the water.

A wave in the sea travels from the speedboat to the shore, but not the actual water. That stays (more or less) in the same place. And a light ray is a wave travelling through the 'electromagnetic' sea which is the universe. So, Einstein wondered, what would it be like to travel at the same speed as a light ray?

Would another light wave then appear to be stationary?

Discussion

But change is essential to light, and indeed any other 'electromagnetic' wave. According to another of Maxwell's theories, it is change in a magnetic field that creates an electrical field, and change in the electrical field that creates magnetism. Some electrical waves create a magnetic field that creates an electrical field that creates . . . The wave that travels through an electromagnetic field at a constant velocity of 186,000 miles a second (300,000 km/s), oscillating between being electrical and magnetic all the time, is the one we know as 'light'. So how could there be such a thing as a 'motionless' light ray?

Einstein decided that if the light wave appeared stationary, then it must cease to exist. In a recourse to empirical evidence, or rather what passes amongst physicists for common sense, he said that no one had ever found a 'spatially oscillatory electromagnetic field at rest'. (Certainly, I have never seen one, and neither has my dog, and we've hunted for one everywhere.) Einstein wrote later:

> From the very beginning it appeared to me intuitively clear that, judged from the standpoint of such an observer, [travelling at the speed of light, relative to the Earth] everything would have to happen according to the same laws as for an observer who, relative to the Earth, was at rest. For how, otherwise, should the first observer know (i.e. be able to determine) that he is in a state of fast uniform motion?

In this lies the germ of the Special Theory of Relativity. Mind you, there's not so much Special about that old theory anyway. Einstein

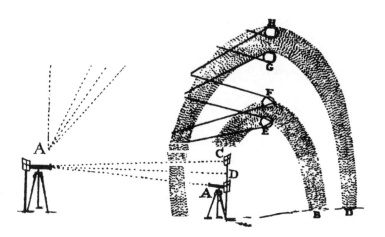

Figure 11   Einstein unravelling light waves

originally called his paper 'The Electrodynamics of Moving Bodies', a much more sensible title, but for some reason it became known as the Special Theory of Relativity. The paper starts with another rather technical sort-of thought experiment too, designed to show that electrodynamics – studies of heat and light and magnetism – can dispense with the need for 'absolute rest', the theory we left dangling in Newton's bucket earlier.

In his experiment Einstein imagines a magnet and a wire spiral moving relative to each other. Doing this creates an electrical current in the wire. (And, unlike racing light waves, you could do this one at home.) But first of all, Einstein imagines the wire moving and the magnet at 'absolute' rest. Doing this, he points out, like a good, if slightly repetitive, master of ceremonies, induces an electrical current in the wire. Then, in the second part of the thought experiment, the wire is stationary and the magnet moves. But doing this also induces an electrical current in the wire.

> Examples of this sort, together with the unsuccessful attempts to discover any motion of the earth relatively to the 'light medium' [the so-called aether supposed to fill space and so 'conduct' light] suggest that the phenomena of electrodynamics as well as of mechanics possess no properties corresponding to the idea of absolute rest.

Instead, in the Special Theory, the first rule is that the speed of light is the same for all observers, regardless of their motion relative to the source of the light. The second 'Salvatius' Ship' one is that anyone (as long as they are not subject to different gravitational or acceleration effects) should observe the same physical laws. Putting these two ideas together, Einstein showed that the only way this can happen is if time and space themselves change. That of course flies against our everyday experience but it has nonetheless been successful at explaining events in more rarified circumstances. For example (and as indicated in experiment T), scientists have shown that an atomic clock flying at high speed in a jet plane will tick more slowly than one left behind at the aerodrome, while during eclipses astronomers have detected starlight being 'bent' by the sun's gravity.

In this case matter interacts with energy, for Einstein's discovery of the relativity of space and time led to another important conclusion. Matter and energy are forever related, as in the famous equation: $E = mc^2$. (Where m = mass and c = the speed of light. Spookily enough, all three are also my initials! But Einstein deserves no credit for that.)

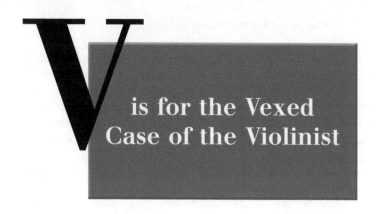

V is for the Vexed Case of the Violinist

SPECIAL EQUIPMENT NEEDED: **an available hospital bed**

Judith Jarvis Thompson asks us to consider the case of the unfortunate pedestrian who wakes up one day to find that they have been kidnapped by members of the desperate Society for Music Lovers, drugged and taken into hospital. There the music lovers have arranged that their prisoner's internal organs be connected via various tubes to a famous violinist whose own organs have failed.

The fact is that disconnecting the violinist now will inevitably kill him. The good news is that the doctors estimate in nine months or so the violinist will be able to survive on his own.

So the question is, if we were in the position of that unfortunate pedestrian, would we agree to stay in the hospital bed . . .

or demand to be 'unplugged' and allowed to continue our lives? Music lovers step aside!

Discussion

It seems the underlying comparison is with a woman who has become pregnant and is told she has an obligation to the unborn child that overrides her own wishes. It's a thought experiment that springs over the much discussed aspect of whether a 'foetus' is really a human being, or at least a 'potential one', to highlight another aspect: the extent to which any individual really has an obligation to save the life of another.

Judith Jarvis Thompson accepts that there is a general moral obligation to save others, but challenges the simplicity of the 'right to life' movement is supposing that this obligation can be considered absolute, and an end to discussion of the matter. The thought experiment shows that we might ourselves hesitate to allow others (the Society for Music Lovers) to impose their judgement of the 'right to life' of the violinist whilst overriding our rights as autonomous human beings.

Some people say that the thought experiment is misleading, even badly designed, in that it compares the 'unborn child' (or, less emotively, the 'foetus') to a human being with full rights. Yet I think this is one of the charms of the thought experiment technique: it sets aside one aspect to allow us to concentrate on another. If we decide that even after we have been kidnapped and connected up, the violinist cannot expect us to 'lie back' and accept the situation, then J. J. Thompson's point is made, and is all the stronger for having been fought on the more difficult ground. On the other hand, if we decide the violinist can demand the use of our liver and so on for nine months, then we can still proceed from there to consider cases where we are connected to something else with less autonomy and fewer rights to see if that makes a difference. (Perhaps a pop singer . . . a rare animal . . . or a philosopher.)

Again, and Judith Thompson explores this aspect in subsequent variations, our kidnapped pedestrian has no personal responsibility for the welfare of the violinist. The comparison is said to be more like that of a victim of rape being required to carry the attacker's child. Indeed, some people will say that a woman who accepts the 'risk' of pregnancy must in so doing accept the duty towards the unborn child. But this is not a great objection to the power of the thought experiment. As a matter of fact, it is a strength. If the debate shifts to the expectations and attitudes of the woman towards the possibility of pregnancy, then it continues to make points.

In setting the parameters for the experiment, Judith Jarvis Thompson concedes the foetus its right to life, but withholds an open-ended commitment to sustaining that life. Instead, the experiment

The Vexed Case of the Violinist

makes the case for the individual woman being the only authority on the matter of whether to provide the life support system of the womb to another. Neither the child (the violinist) – far less the State (the Society for Music Lovers) – have the right to demand it.

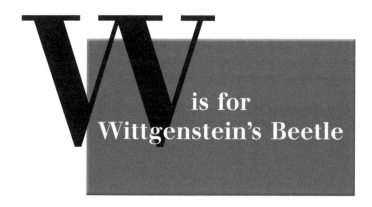

W is for Wittgenstein's Beetle

SPECIAL EQUIPMENT NEEDED: **a matchbox (can be empty)**

In this celebrated thought experiment, that old sceptic of the technique, Wittgenstein, offers another way to consider the nature of language. First of all, the beetle slowly marches across the page . . .

. . . Suppose everyone had a box with something in it: we call it a 'beetle'. No one can look into anyone else's box, and everyone says he knows what a beetle is by looking at his beetle. Here it would be quite possible for everyone to have something different in his box. One might even imagine such a thing constantly changing. But suppose the word 'beetle' had a use in these people's language? If so, it would not be used as the name of a thing. The thing in the box has no place in the language-game at all; not even as a *something*: for the box might even be empty. No one can 'divide through' by the thing in the box; it cancels out, whatever it is. (*Philosophical Investigations*, para. 293)

Wittgenstein's Beetle is supposed to show that people assume that because they are using the same words they are talking about the same thing, when it fact they may be discussing different matters, and what's more, doing so in quite different ways. There is a straightforward parallel between the beetle in the box and, say, 'consciousness' or perhaps a sensation like 'pain' in someone's personal 'beetle box' or 'head'. Everyone has such a sensation. But only they can look at it, and they cannot allow others to 'open the box'.

And the beetle is supposed to be like words and concepts generally. It is supposed to sever the link between concepts in our heads, and things in the world, by way of words. Today, the beetle is claimed by

87

Figure 12 Wittgenstein's menagerie

linguists, doctors and psychologists, artists and aesthetes to radically transform the conventional view of the stability of meaning and language.

Did the beetle just do that?

Discussion

Or is the thought experiment simply flawed in that the supposed conclusion simply does not seem to flow on from the starting assumptions. What would it be like if everyone were born with a beetle to carry around in a secret box? Let us try our own thought experiment using Wittgensteinian 'beetle boxes'!

On a certain island there is a tradition in which everyone is presented at birth with a little 'beetle' box, like a matchbox. These boxes are valued very highly and are very personal things. No one may ever look into another person's box, to see what it contains. Instead, they must content themselves with inspecting what is in their own little box.

Now it so happens that in some of the boxes are big black beetles; in some of them little tiny red ones which are what we would call ants; in some of them are cockroaches. On the island there are no other beetles, ants or for that matter cockroaches, so no one is ever tempted to exclaim: look there goes my beetle! And as it is not permitted (of course) to draw or photograph the contents of your box, the only way people can communicate on the matter is by talking about 'their beetle'.

But this would be enough for comparisons to be made. Someone would look at a red berry and say, that is the colour of my beetle. Someone would look at a coin and say 'that is the size of my beetle' and someone would look at a scurrying spider and say 'that moves like my beetle'. In time a complete picture of the beetles could be communicated and it would become obvious that the beetles in people's boxes were very different.

Thus it will be seen that the Beetle does not provide any support for the many different conclusions claimed by philosophers, psychologists and so many others. If anything, it might even lend itself better to demonstrating the stability of language and communication. A better thought experiment might have produced a better debate.*

On the other hand, it might not.

---

* The beetle is dissected further in the 'How to' section.

X is for Xenophanes and Thinking by Examples

SPECIAL EQUIPMENT NEEDED: **horse or cow that is able to paint**

Homer and Hesiod have attributed to the gods
Everything that men find shameful and reprehensible:
Stealing, adultery, and deceiving one another.
The Ethiopians paint their gods black with a flat nose,
The Thracians with blue eyes and red hair.
And if cows and horses or lions had hands,
Or could draw with their hands and make things as men can,
Horses would have drawn horse-like gods,
Cows cow-like gods,
And each species would have made the gods' bodies just like
*   their own . . .*

                              (*Fragments*, 11–16.)

(On the other hand, as the parody goes, 'If animals believed in God, the Devil would definitely look like a human being.')

Xenophanes was born in Colophon in Ionia some two and half thousand years ago, and spent the greater part of the sixth century BCE as a wandering poet, singing drinking songs and retelling tales of Zeus and the other Greek Gods. Eventually, however, he settled in Elea, southern Italy, and it was there that he founded one of the first schools of philosophy, the Eleatic School, which would later count Parmenides and Zeno amongst its illustrious alumni.

And it was there, in a long philosophical poem known as *On Nature*, that Xenophanes did several important things. First, he challenged the central assumptions of contemporary Greek religion, which on its own was the sort of thing that could lead (and for Socrates, of course, did lead) to being executed. Xenophanes, however, seems to have flourished with his subversion. And secondly, his poem uses a new style of argument, the method of comparison, to illustrate the relationship of the images people construct of their gods to their own characteristics.

Instead of a heavenly free-for-all, Xenophanes has it that that there is but one single and eternal God (preferably sphere-shaped). Thus, according to theologians, introducing 'monotheism' into Western thought – not bad all things considered, for an early, prototype, thought experiment.

Although others would say that since Xenophanes' God is the whole universe, including as a tiny part of it humankind, he is not so much a monotheist as a 'pantheist' – or maybe even an atheist.

Be that as it may, how scientific is his method?

Discussion

Xenophanes is also remembered for having observed fossil fishes and shells, and having concluded that the land where they were found must have been underwater at some time. From this he suggested that the world might have formed from the condensation of water and 'primordial mud'. He further surmised from the existence of fossils that the world evolved from a mixture of earth and water, and that the Earth will gradually be re-dissolved. He believed that the Earth had already gone through this cycle several times.

On other occasions, he observed the Earth's shadow on the moon during eclipses, and concluded that the Earth must have the same shape as its shadow – namely that it must be a perfect circle. Therefore the Earth is not flat, as Empedocles and Anaximenes thought; nor drum-shaped, as Leucippus; nor bowl-shaped, as Heraclitus; nor hollow, as Democritus; nor cylindrical, as Anaximander; nor even does it extend infinitely downward, as Xenophon taught; but it must be a perfect sphere.

So, despite the drinking, in the few fragments that remain of his works Xenophanes shows a remarkably scientific as well as sceptical outlook. But then his background lay with the Milesian school of Ionia founded by Thales, who was famed for successfully predicting the eclipse of 585 BC (and thereby stopping a battle). In another fragment, Xenophanes dismisses the rainbows in which others saw the workings of the Goddess Isis as but 'simply a cloud that appears crimson, red and yellowish green'. Elsewhere, he states that 'men can have no certain knowledge, only opinion' and that although, by searching, people can improve their understanding, this 'will always fall short of knowledge'.

> *The gods did not reveal from the beginning*
> *All things to us; but in the course of time*
> *Through seeking, men found that which is better.*
> *But as for certain truth, no man has known it,*
> *Nor will he know it; neither of the gods,*
> *Nor yet of all the things of which I speak.*
> *And even if by chance he were to utter*
> *The final truth, he would himself not know it;*
> *For all is but a woven web of guesses.*
> (Xenophanes, c.570–470 BCE)

Y is for Counterfactuals and a Backwards Approach to History

SPECIAL EQUIPMENT NEEDED: **packet of spare nails**

The Great Wall of China is one of the wonders of the ancient world, a 'sleeping dragon' that lies in lazy coils from one end of that vast land to the other. It is said to be visible from space, and that if built on a more conventional scale, it would have enough stone to stretch right around the equator.

Yet what if the Chinese had not built such a very Great Wall?

After all, this was a quite ridiculously huge undertaking, perhaps equivalent in money terms to the US's post-war devotion to its own stockpile of weapons. (You could imagine some right-wing historian making something of that.) The Wall might much more plausibly have never happened than have happened.

Yet Qin Shih Huang, the first Emperor, did start the Wall, in the third century BCE, as a way of unifying the 'Middle Kingdom'. It probably bankrupted him, but subsequent rulers extended it nonetheless, both in order to keep out the Huns and as a valuable trade route – the key to the legendary Silk Roads. Most of what exists today is much more recent though, built by the Ming dynasty (1368–1644 CE) who relied on the Wall to protect them from the bloodthirsty Mongols.

There is documentary evidence that the Wall was highly successful in reducing raids, with written records showing many attacks successfully repelled. No border fort was ever taken and held against the wall's defenders. At the same time, when central government in China was weak, the effect on both regional loyalties and the defences themselves meant that on at least two occasions, invasions were successful.

If there had been no Great Wall, it seems likely enough that there would have been no flowering of Chinese culture and invention. And if some in the West shrug at that, it should be realized that that also means that there would have been no intellectual heritage for the West to shamelessly plunder.

Practical inventions such as the iron plough, the first efficient horse harness (and the stirrup), the incredibly effective 'seed drill' are all Chinese. Then there's the chain pump, the suspension bridge, the belt-drive and the key elements of the steam engine. Not to mention the first mechanical clocks, ship's rudders and watertight compartments, and (better acknowledged) inventions like the compass, paper and gunpowder. Not to forget theoretical as much as practical works in astronomy, medicine, printing, mathematics and last (but not least) philosophy.

Without the Great Wall wouldn't barbarian hordes have swept regularly over the Chinese landscape, reducing towns and cities to the cultural level of the northern steppe, where the height of sophistication was seen as playing polo with a dead enemy's head?

It's a bit of a shocker, but without the Great Wall might there never even have been the flowering of Ancient Greece and philosophy?

Discussion

History has proved fertile ground for the imaginings. It is not only in the creative interpretation of facts, that historians use their imagination, nor even in the surreptitious invention of missing ones, but these days in the full-blown 'literary' exercise of composing a new historical narrative. And (for us) the most interesting form of this, as well as perhaps the most structured form, is that of the historical counterfactual.

These are stories which beg to be awarded some sort of factual status, without actually needing to have happened. They are instead things that *could* have happened. What if the Greeks had lost at Marathon? If Hitler had won the war? If human beings were allergic to meat? Or if the twentieth-century Communist experiment had succeeded?

Now philosophers have long been concerned with this subtle question of what is 'possible' as opposed to what is flatly impossible. And many philosophers hold that if something is possible then in some sense it already is part of the world of existence. Equally, if diametrically opposed, some philosophers say that 'facts' are created by people, so that they have no great status. Only things that are self-contradictory need to be distinguished, and in the case of a historical 'counterfactual', avoided.

Economists, for instance, interpret the question of 'what is possible' as a dynamic one, depending on the identification of various stable states for the economy. Marx and Engels constructed their 'science of materialism' on the assumption that there was a pattern to history, indeed an inevitable one. In an 1894 letter, Engels wrote 'societies are governed by necessity, the complement and form of appearance of which is accident.' Many today, although denying the Marxists their dream, still see a pattern – usually a 'progression' – to the sequence of historical accidents. (Although, at the same time, there is an important counter-tradition from Jean-Jacques Rousseau to Karl Popper of bemoaning such 'historicism' as introversion and complacency.)

Geographers use similar notions too when they talk, for example, of the earth having a tendency to return to its frozen state, with the ice and snow reflecting sunlight back into space, or speculate about rises in global temperatures.

Now the art of a successful counterfactual is not to suppose something odd and then draw equally bizarre conclusions, but to suppose something odd and draw very plausible conclusions. The idea is that in history, as in economics, climate change or whatever, small events can have great consequences. Working through these in the imagination, the effect of the small invented happening reveals and expands our understandings of more solid and timeless mechanisms.

A Backwards Approach to History

George Herbert's ditty about the horseshoe sums up the approach:

For want of a nail the shoe is lost,
For want of a shoe the horse is lost,
For want of a horse, the rider is lost,
For want of a rider the battle is lost,
For want of a battle the war is lost,
All for want of horseshoe nail.

This gives the attractive feel of a good counterfactual, with a small event operating, as one writer put it, a bit like a nineteenth-century railway points lever – switching the train of history with barely a jolt from one path to another. But back to our own 'switch', our Great Wall 'counterfactual'. Would civilization really have been derailed without it?

It's tempting perhaps to say 'delayed' rather than 'derailed', but one of the greatest historians, R. H. Tawny, wrote that history gives an appearance of inevitability, dragging into prominence the forces which have triumphed and shovelling into the background those which events have swallowed up. Perhaps in this case, the fact of the Great Wall has swallowed up the tendency of the human race to destroy its highest achievements.

Z is for Zeno and the Mysteries of Infinity

SPECIAL EQUIPMENT NEEDED: **book on thought experiments**

Zeno, philosopher of tortoises and runners, challenger of common sense and atomism, is one of the first great thought experimenters.

As everyone knows, Zeno imagined a race between a tortoise and Achilles. The tortoise is given a very generous start, from the half-way mark. Clearly Achilles needs first of all to run to where the tortoise was, before he can catch up. And no matter how slowly the tortoise plods, during that time it will definitely move a little further along the course.

If the lead is now only a few feet, no matter, Achilles must still make that up too. And by the time he has, the tortoise will have moved on again, even if only by a few inches. And so on, for an infinity of ever-diminishing steps . . . On the face of it, Achilles cannot make up the distance.

It is a ridiculous note to end on. Anyway, it was solved years ago.

Or was it?

Discussion

The race has caused philosophers lots of angst over the centuries. Aristotle attempted to deny the tactic of dividing up things into little bits in this way. He thought that yes, *space* could be divided up into ever smaller parts, but that time should be treated as a smooth continuum with Achilles able to sweep past the tortoise as a desirable consequence.

Others have appealed to mathematics, in particular the ability to say that the sum of an infinite series can be a finite number, as long as the numbers are shrinking in size. Here Achilles needs to run something like one-half of the course plus a little bit, 1/128, 1/8192 ... to catch his opponent, and the infinite series – in maths at least – will eventually be a great deal less than 1, so that in the race, Achilles will indeed most likely sweep past his four-legged opponent, and most likely before the three-quarters mark. But those appealing to mathematics may as well appeal to the history of actual races between athletes and tortoises. Zeno *knew* that tortoises were not good at running races – his point is that common-sense assumptions about infinity and divisibility lead to absurd conclusions. And

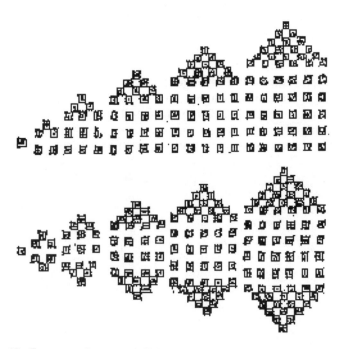

Figure 13 Zeno counting up to infinity

his opponents forget that what is possible in maths is no more certain than the assumptions inevitably made to start with.

Zeno's riddle was not whether tortoises are hard to catch up, but that our common sense and very fundamental notions of space, time and infinity are rather shaky. And that is as true today as it has ever been.

This brings us back to the question posed by Lucretius, in throwing his spear, 'What is the universe itself "in"?'

And that question (which is also one Zeno himself posed) is not so easy to answer. Theoretical physicists today consider us to inhabit an actually or effectively infinite universe. Because of their assumption that there is a finite speed to the transmission of 'information' (the speed of light), it seems to follow that in that case we may live in a kind of 'Hubble Bubble', a mini-universe defined by the distance light could have travelled since its coming into existence – surrounded by an infinity of other 'parallel universes' all in their own Hubble Bubbles.

In these 'other worlds', all possible arrangements of matter exist, conjured into being simply by the effects of probability and infinite occurrence. In fact, in some parallel universe, according to Max Tegmark, a Professor of Physics (so he should know, even if he has not yet found bits of it to put in wooden boxes in his storeroom), there is an exact copy of you in one of these universes reading an exact copy of this book – except that for some reason, you are still on 'G for Galileo', having lost the thread of the book somewhere about there. (Fortunately in other universes there are copies of you (with green hair) who are already contentedly putting away the book having made light work of 'Z'.)

It seems (not to put too fine a point on it) rather a silly theory. I'd rather imagine the tortoise winning the race. But Max is undaunted by such common sense. He points out that it is actually far simpler to assume a cosmos like this, where everything possible exists all the time, than to devise complicated explanations and theories to produce a cosmos that resembles the one we 'just happen to inhabit'.

In a sense, physics has come full circle. It now rejoins philosophy where it started, with a 'metaphysical' view of reality. For by their very nature, such theories cannot be tested. The parallel universes must remain forever hidden, perhaps deducible but never observable. If the fundamental nature of matter too turns out to be unobservable, perhaps an energy wave, flicking sub-atomic particles in and out of existence forever, creating the impression of solidity out of nothing, then the elusive 'theory of everything' that scientists and philosophers (by their different paths) have for so long sought, may turn out to be quite beyond all experiments – *except those of the thought kind.*

Notes for Experimenters

How to Experiment

Seven Laboratory Rules

Well, that's it. I've used a broad brush here to paint my picture of the thought experiment technique. Some people might even say I've used a floor brush, but at least we've covered a lot of ground if so . . . We've seen what a thought experiment is, where to find them, how they've been used, and why. But still the question needs to be answered: what makes a good thought experiment? We have now seen a great many and must decide.

I would say that a good thought experiment should be:

* short and immediately comprehensible;
* transparent, its workings open to scrutiny (without relying on hidden tricks for its effect, or sneaked in bizarre assumptions in order to make it work);
* and definitive, that is, the experiment should be possible to repeat without different results sometimes occurring.

One key feature of all experiments (after all) is that they should produce a result. And, in a well-designed one, the data produced will be unambiguous. It is for that reason that conventional experiments take place 'in the laboratory', where other factors may be more easily eliminated and excluded – factors that might otherwise hide relationships or produce misleading results. Otherwise more experiments will be needed and, in 'real' science at least, that's not a good thing.

Then a good experiment's workings need to be open to inspection, need to be transparent and uncontroversial. Thought experimenters must be careful with their ingredients too, if their work is to be 'replicable'. Their assumptions cannot be peculiar to any one person, or even to one frame of mind. Along with this, the process of the experiment will need to be open to inspection, documented and recorded, otherwise critics may say that another factor, another 'variable', has been allowed to slip unnoticed into the laboratory of the mind, where it has gone on to influence the findings. They may complain that an assumption was faulty or 'contaminated'. But these are precisely the kinds of things that the thought experimenter must be prepared to clarify, debate and justify.

Thought experiments then will carry greater weight: they may even demand acceptance, and refuse to be subject to challenge by future re-run experiments. That was the claim of one of the most celebrated of them all – experiment G, Galileo's Gravitational Balls. For me at least, out of all the A–Z, it is the defining, the 'paradigm' example of a thought experiment. It satisfies all the requirements: it is short and comprehensible (we can all imagine carrying two objects up a tower and throwing them over the side), and its workings are transparent. If there are hidden assumptions, notwithstanding certain philosophical critics, I would not call them 'tricks', and they scarcely merit being called 'bizarre'. Although some philosophers have indeed, as we saw, objected that 'the objects are assumed to drop through the air and not through liquid', or that tiny differences of the earth's gravitational field have been neglected, and so on, it may be such critics perhaps understand science less than they imagine. At least for the rest of us, the conclusion is 'certain', because there are no other possible 'outcomes' to be imagined by future experimenters. Once the balls are connected, then the logical process has its own logic, momentum and power.

Contrast Galileo's Balls with John Searle's Rule-Ruled Room (experiment R). As a thought experiment it is admirably concise and immediately comprehensible. Yet its workings are anything but transparent. To make sense of it we have to introduce all sorts of 'hidden assumptions': about the scope and usage of terms, about meaning, about machines, about language. Small wonder that it has spawned so many 'counter-experiments' and so little agreement. Or, perhaps, we might uncrumple from the laboratory dustbin (for experiments not included in our A–Z) the tale of Peter Strawson's 'world of sounds'. Here the experimenter is asked to imagine a world in which (as he puts it) 'the spatial location of a particular sound is determined by the gradually changing pitch of a master-sound.' We are instructed that when a sound is heard together with a certain pitch of the master-sound, it fixes its location. (A bit like a lost remote control bleeping from behind the back of the sofa, I imagine.) The experiment is supposed to demonstrate that 'place' can be defined without using any 'spatial' criteria.

Now I would be concerned that this (although much admired) thought experiment actually fails all three tests. It is acceptably short, yes, but not immediately (if at all) comprehensible. Indeed, in line with this flaw, there are some very strange assumptions lurking. As several critics complained, in the world of sounds it would seem difficult to distinguish several different objects located together as determined 'by the master-sound', whereas (in the everyday world of things) we can make sense of several different spatial objects being perceived together.

Others have objected too that there is no reason to accept the experiment's distinction between individual 'objective sounds' and 'objective sound-processes'. That sounds are not capable of being split up like this, since they have only 'secondary' perceptual qualities (like duration and volume) and none of the 'primary', enduring qualities (like hardness and what everyone, except Descartes, meant by 'extension'; Descartes, in a sort of little thought experiment, complained that even a rock lacked hardness and extension, as it could be ground up into a fine mush, and yet still remain 'a rock'). The smuggled element in the world of sounds, the critics say, is that before Professor Strawson can place one of his 'perceptual particulars' in it, he must first of all sneak in an 'enduring physical object' to produce the sound.

Actually I'm not sure what to make of all this, and sadly it is true that much that passes in philosophical, let alone scientific debate proper, goes over my head. But one of the charms of the thought experiment is that it at least is supposed to be instantly comprehensible. Otherwise it is not serving its purpose. Obscurity of expression, as the saying goes, may be pardonable, but obscurity of thought experiment is not.

So rule number 1 for thought experimenters is: keep it simple.

The concern with thought experiments like the 'world of sounds', is simply that they are already confusing and untidy – before any conclusions have even started to be drawn. Amidst wrangling about the 'reality' or more precisely the 'conceivability', they begin to fall apart. For philosophers know only too well that to be 'inconceivable' is to be doomed, like 'round squares' and 'selfless politicians', to non-existence. It was for that reason that Mr Descartes spent considerable periods of time musing in his medieval oven in order to produce the 'inconceivability' of a thought without a thinker, and hence the certainty of existence.

Rule 2 of thought experiments is that they must be possible to imagine.

The clearer the picture, the stronger the image, the better the experiment. Yet sometimes the image is strong, but misleading. Take Wittgenstein's Beetle (experiment W), for instance. Here the experiment appears straightforward enough, but (gnawed away at by ontological doubts) fails to offer any guidance. It falls, as it were, at the third hurdle. But let's look again at Wittgenstein's famous thought experiment, to see the thought experiment technique being used (abused) recently in practice.

Wittgenstein's Beetle and the risks of experimentation built upon shaky foundations

Wittgenstein's Beetle is supposed to show that people assume that because they are using the same words they are talking about the same thing, whereas in fact they can quite often be discussing quite different matters in quite different ways. As we saw in the A–Z, a parallel is drawn between the beetle in the box and 'consciousness' or, perhaps, a sensation like 'pain' in someone's personal 'beetle box' or 'head'. Everyone has such sensations. But only they can look at them, and they cannot allow others to 'open the box'.

Let us eavesdrop first of all on the social scientists (psychologists) using the thought experiment technique recently at www.bioethics.gov:

DR ELLIOTT: (*Intends to show the arbitrary nature of words like 'pain'*) I have a sort of thought experiment here that I want to repeat to you. It comes from Wittgenstein. Whenever I say the word 'Wittgenstein' people's eyes tend to glaze over. So I'll make it short.

PROF SANDEL: Here they brighten.
   (*Laughter*)

DR ELLIOTT: I'll look at you then! Okay . . . There's a famous passage in the *Philosophical Investigations*, the so-called Beetle Box game where Wittgenstein says imagine a game.[1] Suppose everybody has a box. Something is in it. We call it a beetle, 'beetle' in scare quotes here, a beetle. Nobody else can look into anyone else's box.

   Everyone says he knows what a beetle is only by looking at his beetle. Right? Now, Wittgenstein says, look. It would be quite possible for each person to have something different in his box. In fact, it would

---

[1] Philosophical *ingenues* should be aware that at least the 'later' Wittgenstein argued that language is a kind of game played by humans.

even be possible for the contents of the boxes to be constantly changing. In fact, it would even be possible for all [or some] of the boxes to be empty. Yet still the players could still use that term 'beetle' to refer to the contents of their boxes. There don't have to be any actual beetles in the boxes for the game to be played.

Get to the point, please, doctor!

DR ELLIOTT: Now, what's the point, you're asking yourself. Well, the point is that the words that we use to describe our inner lives, our psychological states, words like 'depression' or 'anxiety' or 'fulfilment,' those words get their meanings not by referring and pointing to intermental [*sic*] states, things in our heads. They get their meaning from the rules of the game, the social context in which they're used.

They're like the word 'beetle' in Wittgenstein's game. We learn how to use the words not by looking inward and naming what we see there. We learn how to use the words by playing the game. *The players don't all need to be experiencing the same thing in order for the words to make sense.*

I say I am fulfilled. You say you're fulfilled. We both understand what the other means. Yet that doesn't mean that our inner psychic states are the same. Right? We can all talk about our beetles, yet still have different things in our boxes. . . .

Did the beetle experiment do all that? Yet, if it did, the same thought experiment brought some Russian philosophers to a different conclusion. In fact, it turns out, for the Russians, that the Beetle's message is quite the reverse and that really the very notion of 'a private language in which a person talks about private sensations' is meaningless. This is because, as they put it:

According to Wittgenstein, since language is a social game it requires more than one player. The notion of a rule is fundamental to language, and a private rule is meaningless.

The beetle seems to have partially gnawed its way out of its box. But now here is another philosopher, James Still, taking up the magnifying glass to examine the beetle's trail. 'In the end, we don't seem to know what, if anything, is inside of someone else's beetle box, at least not when we insist on holding to the theory that sensations are known only in our own cases', he explains earnestly if somewhat tautologically, before continuing:

How to Experiment

What I find interesting here is that Wittgenstein does not deny that
... pain-behavior may be accompanied by real pain. It seems that what
he is denying is the existence of a 'criterion of correctness' and the
verification of *sensation S* by our use of the verbs 'to know' and 'to
understand.'

Now the beetle is hiding again in its matchbox. But fortunately,
Garth Kemerling (on a nearby website) takes up the issue. Evidently
in blissful ignorance of our alternative Beetle experiment, he agrees
that one of the distinctive characteristics of the thought experiment
genus 'Beetle', is that 'there is no way to establish a non-linguistic
similarity between the contents of my own box and those of anyone
else's'. He then appears to have some doubts:

> If any of my experiences were entirely private, then the pain that I feel
> would surely be among them. Yet other people commonly are said to
> know when I am in pain. Indeed, Wittgenstein pointed out that I would
> never have learned the meaning of the word 'pain' without the aid
> of other people, none of whom have access to the supposed private
> sensations of pain that I feel. For the word 'pain' to have any meaning
> at all presupposes some sort of external verification, a set of criteria
> for its correct application, and they must be accessible to others as
> well as to myself.

Meanwhile however, at 'ludwig online', one correspondent has gone
back to basics.

> The contents of the box are only for the person holding it to look at so
> it is quite possible that although everyone has what he or she calls a
> 'beetle', each beetle is really something entirely different from anyone
> else's beetle. Although the word functions in the language of this group
> of people, it does not have a consistently corresponding meaning and
> therefore does not play a part in their language game, not even as a
> something; *for the box might even be empty.*

But if the box is empty – what has happened to the beetle? Please
explain! And it seems that although the word 'beetle' may have meaning to each box-holder, it does not acquire that meaning through
reference to what is actually in the box.

> A private sensation is not a something, but he [Wittgenstein] insists
> elsewhere that it is not a nothing either. The conclusion was only that
> a nothing (the empty box) would serve just as well as a something
> about which nothing can be said. We have only rejected the grammar
> that is forced upon us here.

How to Experiment

Quite, I feel the same way. A nothing would serve just as well as a something about which nothing can be said. And it seems sadly to be that many thought experiments qualify as 'a something' about which nothing can be said. No doubt many 'Wittgensteinians', 'Strawsonions' and so on would want to rush in and deny that their mentors' work should even be interpreted as 'thought experimentation', but rather as 'analogies' to help those unable to follow some supposed more rigorous formal argument. But analogies are ill-defined things that bear some resemblance to other things, yet only in some respects. They can provide illustrations or examples, never any real insights.

And that thought experiments are more than mere illustrations is reflected by the trouble philosophers and scientists alike go to in producing and then vigourously rebutting 'counter-examples'. Wittgensteinians, for example, would no doubt decry the one offered in experiment W, for requiring the perception of a red berry in one person's 'beetle box' (that is at this point their 'head') to be the same as that in another's. 'Ah ha!' they may shout excitedly. 'But that is just the point! No one can explain anything without assuming some shared concepts or ideas – and there may be none at all!'

Indeed, there is a whole literature on Wittgenstein's so-called Private Language Argument, in which a few cryptic Wittgensteinisms (like the Beetle experiment) are dissected, mulled over and prodded for signs of life.

The words of this language are to refer to what can be known only to the speaker; to his immediate, private sensations. So another cannot understand the language. (*Philosophical Investigations*)

A substantial body of work, including new thought experiments produced by philosophers (such as Saul Kripke) has built up, all striving to present a definitive interpretation of what Wittgenstein meant. But at the end of the day, each new version relies upon the introduction of extra assumptions and material, because the original accounts are just too sparse and too ambiguous to lead to any conclusion.

Rule 3 is: thought experiments should contain a complete argument.

The Beetle thought experiment is set in a world in which there is some sort of settled, shared knowledge, language, perception – because, for example, people all know what a beetle box (that is at this point now a matchbox again) is. At the end of it though, the Wittgenstein beetle boxes are being carried around in a world of which nothing can ultimately be known. The experimenter might be challenged, quite what purpose is served by picking out the contents of the boxes as especially mysterious? (Certainly, when a thought experiment assumes this sort of settled shared world, it cannot then be withdrawn, willy-nilly, by supporters of the experiment determined to bolster its findings.)

Rule 5 is that things must be consistent. No one likes discrepancies.

What is ruled out in one part cannot be snuck back in somewhere else ... It seems that is why our psychologists wish to make a special case for 'mental sensations' as somehow more 'subjective' than say, sense perception, but in that case, the problem is, as the philosophers pointed out long ago, that really all our knowledge is one step removed from reality. (And sometimes more than one.)

John Locke sums sums up the ancient debate in *An Essay Concerning Human Understanding* (1690). Real essence, he explains there, 'may be taken for the very being of anything, whereby it is what it is' and the 'real internal, but generally (in substances) unknown constitution of things, whereon their discoverable qualities depend'. Nominal essence, on the other hand, may be taken for 'that abstract idea which the general ... name stands for' (Book II, iii, 15).

The question though is: attractive as Wittgenstein's imaginary beetle indubitably is, or as Searle's Chinese Room, or even Professor Strawson's 'purely auditory world' may be, especially for those searching for something tangible in a discussion of intangibles – do such experiments offer real, or merely misleading, simplifications? Do the experiments take us nearer or further from understanding the issue?

Not that is it easy to think of good thought experiments. If philosophers seem sometimes to suck the blood out of the few that there are, they must be forgiven when we remember the difficulties of constructing new, let alone, useful ones.

Rule 6 is: don't let the story run away with the plot.

And this issue of the misleading simplification, the ingenious but irrelevant comparison, applies even to the most practical issues. As was mentioned in the introduction, the contemporary philosopher, Tamara Horowitz, has said that 'rescue dilemmas', such as ones about rescuing people in danger of drowning or burning in buildings, are misleading. In one simple incarnation, a solitary person is in one place and five other people are in another, and the rescuers can't get to both locations. She takes issue with those (like Warren Quinn) who think that to 'fail to save' the solitary person is 'justified'. After all, she says, if the thought experiment is adjusted so that you can only save the five by 'driving over and thereby killing someone who is trapped on the road' then the same (previously content) people say that it would be 'far from obvious' that it is right to do so – and yet the 'only thing' that has been changed is the language!

Well, such is the bread and butter of thought experiments in ethics. But Tamara Horowitz's objection is also very germane to the issues we have been looking at. That the language used in the examples influences you is a useful enough observation to be sure, and one backed up in this case with an impressive sequence of graphs and diagrams. And to underline the point, she cites a 'real' experiment involving the (deliberately) incompetent application of the thought experiment technique. In one room, a group of people are asked to consider a dilemma involving 'Asian flu' and lots of victims with varying chances under varying scenarios of 'being saved'. Meanwhile, in a second room, a similar group are consulted on the advisability of exactly the same scenarios, but with the figures emphasizing instead the numbers of people each scenario would kill.

The experts, two psychologists, Daniel Kahneman and Amos Tversky, found that people were influenced by the wording used. They would vote in favour of immunization programmes to *save* people from diseases, but against programmes in which they are told a lot of people 'will die' – even when in numerical terms the two strategies are equivalent.

In one sense, their test illustrates what economists have long noted, namely that people worry about losses more than gains, but Tamara Horowitz uses it rather to conclude that responses to ethical thought experiments (in particular) are greatly influenced by what she terms the 'framing' of the question. And that is certainly something we must be aware of in designing our own ones.

Rule 7 is: you must be careful about the words you choose.

That's one concern. Another effect of framing questions is more subtle, but even more dangerous. Consider this problem, for example, told to me by one of philosophy's most original Yorkshire Cypriot exponents, Zenon Stavrinides. (And how's that for 'framing'?)

Zenon recounts how he was driving along a remote road in the Yorkshire Dales on his motorbike on a wild, stormy night, when he passed by a desolate bus stop, and saw three people huddling in it, waiting in vain for the bus. (He actually saw it pass by ahead earlier.) Zenon stops, and asks who would like a lift. It turns out they all have a good claim for his help . . .

How to Experiment

The first to speak is an old lady who looks as if she is about to die, and says she needs to get to the hospital urgently . . .

The second is a healthy looking middle-aged man who it turns out is an old friend. He once saved Zenon's life, and now needs to get to town or he will lose his job . . .

And the last? The last is a beautiful woman, whom Zenon immediately and intuitively realizes is the perfect partner of his dreams – and what's more, it is obvious that the woman thinks the same thing.

Yet he can only carry one passenger on his motorbike.

That's the experiment. It's clear, it's possible and it has at least some ethical import. The question now is, which one of the three deserving cases would you choose to offer a ride to, knowing that there could only be one passenger on the motorbike?

As Zenon says, Think! before you continue reading . . .

You could pick up the old lady, because she is going to die and thus you should save her first; or, you could take the old friend because he once saved your life and this would be the perfect chance to pay him back. One's a 'right' and the other's a sort-of duty . . . However, do either of those deeds and you may never be able to find your 'once in a lifetime' perfect partner again – and isn't your (her?) happiness worth something too?

This is a dilemma that was once, apparently, used as part of a job application. The candidate who was ostensibly appointed had no trouble coming up with his answer, simply saying: 'I would give the keys to my old friend and let him take the lady to the hospital. Meanwhile, I would stay behind and wait on the desolate road with the partner of my dreams.'

The moral is that sometimes we gain more if we are able to give up our stubborn thought limitations. Never forget to 'think outside of the box', even in a carefully constructed experiment.

So now, what is it that makes a useful thought experiment anyway? Certainly they are more than the sum of their parts – they do perform some work. We must distinguish them from the theoretical examples which abound in philosophy, like currants in a stodgy pudding. Examples, after all, as mentioned above, are no more than pictures, requiring not so much active interpretation as passive contemplation. Analogies are unreliable. And while philosophy problems certainly require thought, they offer few indications as to just how such thought is to be directed. Worst of all, they frequently make their living, in philosophical circles at least, by being reliably 'insoluble'. Philosophy problems, like philosophers themselves, survive on ambiguity. But thought experiments are supposed to illuminate and even offer solutions to the problems.

The best of the riddles of philosophy and logic, however, such as the race between Achilles and the tortoise, or the question of whether we can believe a Cretan who tells us that all Cretans are liars, also serve a purpose: they are there to highlight complexities, or as Plato put it, to 'sting us' into an awareness that there are things that we do not know and cannot explain. We should not be too dismissive of our philosophical concerns, despite their veneer of practicality, there is this same use for thought experiments too. They may be dubious in their 'simplifications', debatable in their allegories, yet like the Beetle, if they have proved fruitful in provoking responses and extending debate then they have served a purpose.

As Thomas Kuhn, the philosopher who advocated the power of 'paradigm shifts', puts it in *A Function for Thought Experiments* (1977), they can also provide new information not so much about the world, but about our conceptual apparatus and understandings. But thought experiments do, at least on occasion, make a rather more striking claim: that they have this mysterious ability to actually add to our knowledge of the world without needing to directly engage with it. It is this which has, as we saw in the introduction, left so many puzzled if not downright suspicious of the technique.

Yet Thomas Kuhn's idea offers a clue. He says that the claims made in thought experiments are a kind of linguistic mathematics, in which known relationships are expressed, put alongside each other and then 'solved'. Perhaps then, we might add, in the manner of solving simultaneous equations. The individual equations may not say much on their own, but set methodically alongside each other, real findings may be made.

This leads to an idea for another way to think about thought experiments: to conceptualize the technique, as it were. A sort of thought experiment on thought experiments?

The Grasshopper (for non-mathematicians)

Suppose we have a rather small puzzle with a mathematical flavour (like so many thought experiments) like this: Some scientists are trying to find the weight of a grasshopper as compared to a cicada without hurting the insects (this last requirement being rather unusual in laboratories). The problem is that the insects keep jumping on and off the scales and refuse to sit there patiently, so that after many attempts at weighing them they have still only found out that one grasshopper and two cicada weigh 7 grams in little weights. But how much does a grasshopper weigh?

Being trained to be systematic, they pose the question as:

$$g + 2c = 7 \qquad g = ?$$

But it is rather hard to tell. They could persist with trying to make just one grasshopper sit on the scales long enough to get its weight. But then one recalls from earlier efforts that:

Two grasshoppers weigh the same as one cicada and 4 grams in weight, or $2g = c + 4$.

Clearly, further practical efforts are unnecessary! Bits of incomplete information can increase in value when put together in a new way.

Mathematical drop-outs may however ask, so? What now is *g*? Well, if we put the two equations together, remembering that you can do anything you like to an equation as long as you do it 'equally' to both sides, we obtain:

$$2g + 4c = 14 \text{ and } 2g = c + 4$$

We only need to make the two equations look the same. The first equation can be expressed instead as $2g = 14 - 4c$ (taking 4c from each side), which is compared with $2g = c + 4$. Clearly then: $14 - 4c = c + 4$. (The reader must solve this one as homework.[2])

So from two pieces of information (which taken separately yielded only confusion) we have obtained new information 'about the world' (inasmuch as the example is based on some real measurements, which it isn't really) just by thinking about the matter a bit. And maths seems to be the key to understanding the physical universe, just as the Ancient Greeks thought.

So, back to our larger question, that of defining 'thought experiments' themselves. One contemporary academic, Ian Ground, who has taught courses on such things, and even raised the issue on the Internet, has suggested (adventurously) that the answer is 'not easy to pin down exactly' but that thought experiments are intended to:

[2] Cicadas weigh 2 grams and grasshoppers weigh 3 grams.

either
- test our intuitions,

or
- reveal assumptions in our thinking.

I would rather say, on the other hand, that they are intended to both:

- test out certain assumptions, through imagining a series of logically implied consequences;
- employ intuition to discover new information and create new relationships.

This in a way is not all that different from 'real' experiments. They too test assumptions and they too rely on an intuitive stage in the design and origination of the experiments, although instead of 'thought' leading the scientist to a conclusion, events are observed and empirical measurements are made. The thought experimenter creates the apparatus out of words by describing the scenario and (like good scientists) outlining their assumptions. Their apparatus still needs to be set up, the ingredients still need to be supplied, even though the experiment ultimately proceeds courtesy of the power of imagination (guided by logic) when they begin to ask what will happen if . . .

Sometimes the suppositions are impossible (at least at present anyway). Plato's story of Gyges, the shepherd who discovers a magic ring that confers invisibility and becomes a bit of a rogue, is not exactly plausible in the mechanism, but it still carries conviction in the aspects relating to the corrupting effects of power and secrecy. Descartes' raising the possibility as to whether the man in the street he can see from his window is really an early automaton moved by wires and levers is similarly not so very likely (but equally not so impossible). For every implausible Poincaré's planet experiment, there are others, such as dropping balls from the leaning tower of Pisa or spinning a bucket around, which could be carried out, and yet (and here is the mark of a good thought experiment) are simply not worth bothering to.

Strangely, it seems people often imagine that many historical thought experiments *were* carried out, but the point is that, like the purest of pure analytical philosophy, thought alone was sufficient to yield certainty. At the finish, it comes down to the fact that the distinction between a thought experiment and a 'real' experiment itself is not so great, and certainly not so unambiguous as at first it seems. The findings of 'real' experiments are not even themselves more 'real': a 'real' experiment is just as open to challenge, its results always only provisional and temporary, until others have confirmed them. And long afterwards, as the history of science well shows, these findings may yet still be overturned as a new theory exposes theoretical inconsistencies on the grand scale, or experimenter bias or ignorance on the smaller. For facts follow theories, and not vice versa.

For that reason at least then, in both earthly and imaginary laboratories the reality is that the questions remain still more interesting and more important than the answers.

Notes and Cuttings

Further reading on Deep Thought: a brief history

Aristotle's 'lance' theory is set out in *Physics*, Book IV, viii. Roger Wertheimer's experiment is in 'Understanding the Abortion Argument', published in *Philosophy and Public Affairs* (1971). Tamara Horowitz's views are set out in 'Philosophical Intuitions and Psychological Theory', in *Ethics* (vol. 108, January 1998) while Warren Quinn is writing in *Morality and Action* on 'Actions and Consequences: The Doctrine of Doing and Allowing' (Cambridge University Press, 1993). Daniel Dennett's paper on 'Artificial Life' was for the inaugural issue of the journal *Artificial Life* in 1994. Anthony Quinton was writing in *The Soul in Personal Identity*, edited by John Perry (University of Berkeley, 1975). Jonathan Dancy's paper, 'The Role of Imaginary Cases in Ethics', was for the *Pacific Philosophical Quarterly* (1985).

Sissela Bok's book *Secrets: On the Ethics of Concealment and Revelation* was published by Vintage in 1983. Alan Shewmon asked his medical question in 'The Metaphysics of Brain Death, Persistent Vegetative State, and Dementia', published in *The Thomist* in 1985.

The Einstein quote on the limits of mathematics is from his paper entitled 'Geometry and Experience', while the 'elevator' or moving box experiment was first described in 'Gravitational Problems', 1912 (pp. 1254–5).

The contemporary philosopher Peter King has made a particular study of common-sense medieval thought experiments, and claims that 'it was "obvious" that a large stone will hit the ground before a small one', and hence that Galileo must have actually tried his famous 'leaning tower of Pisa' experiment out (see experiment G). In fact, he challenges the scientists too with his opinion that 'theoretical physics, no matter how theoretical, qualifies as physics for us in virtue of being hooked up to experimental testing in the long run.' The debate can be perused on page 46 of *Thought Experiments in Science and Philosophy*, edited by Tamara Horowitz and Gerald Massey (Rowman & Littlefield, 1991), which is full of erudite stuff on many of the issues in this chapter.

Not particularly recommended, but for those who like such things, Peter Strawson's book *Individuals* (Methuen, 1959) contains the 'world of sounds' thought experiment.

Finally, the Wittgenstein quote here is from the *Blue and Brown Books* (Blackwell, 1958) pp. 61–2.

Further reading on the debate over thought experiments in general

Two of the relatively rare philosohical discussions of thought experiments are James Brown's *The Laboratory of the Mind* (Routledge, 1991) and Roy Sorenson's business-like monograph, *Thought Experiments* (Oxford University Press, 1992). Both dwell extensively on scientific matters and are aloof to the wider range of the technique.

Further reading on the A–Z

A: Alice and Acceleration

Francis Bacon (1561–1626) discusses the matter in 'The Advancement of Learning', published in 1605.

Galileo is writing in *Dialogo dei Massimi Sistemi* (Giornata Seconda, Florence edition of 1842, vol. 1, pp. 251–2).

Physicists refer to this as the 'Cannon ball problem', and an article by Larry Gedney of the Geophysical Institute, Alaska, discussing the issue in all its full technical complexity, is on the Internet at www.gi.alaska.edu. Another curious fact is that the time taken to fall through the centre of the earth to the other side, and bounce back up again, should be exactly the same as the time taken to orbit the earth.

The illustrated account of 'A Hole through the Earth', by the French astronomer Camille Flammarion, can be found in *The Strand Magazine*, vol. 38 (1909), p. 348. 'Maglev' is, of course, short for 'magnetic levitation' – the very expensive kind of trains in search of a purpose, that are nonetheless already being built and whizzed along tracks suspended in mid air by the forces of electromagnetism, and I should also give acknowledgements here to *The Annotated Alice* (Random

Notes and Cuttings

House, 1998), Lewis Carroll, introduction and notes by Martin Gardner, and in particular chapter 1 'Down the Rabbit Hole'.

B: the Body/Mind-Transfer Machine

This is a popular thought experiment! There are many books and papers to read, but consider particularly René Descartes in the first of his *Meditations* – the body is divisible, the mind is not, and David Hume, *Of Human Nature*, especially Treatise 1 where he observes that the lumpy oyster has no notion of self.

Bernard Williams' 'The Self and the Future', in *Personal Identity*, edited by John Perry, (University of Berkeley, 1975) also discusses some of the philosophical problems with the machine.

You could try *The Philosophy and Psychology of Personal Identity* by Jonathan Glover (Penguin, 1988), including multiple personalities, and 'doubling', but only zealots need bother with *Real People: Personal Identity Without Thought Experiments,* by Kathleen V. Wilkes (Clarendon Press, 1993). Derek Parfit's *Reasons and Persons* (Clarendon Press, 1984) has a virtual hospital of thought experiments including multiplexing minds, hemispherectomies, and potions to induce irrational behaviour. (Other than beer, that is.)

C: the Cannibal

From Bertrand Russell, *History of Western Philosophy* and St Thomas Aquinas, Book IV of the *Summa Contra Gentiles*. Epicurus (341–270 BCE), although his name is loosely associated with 'pleasure', was actually more precisely into 'sensation'. Hence his view of death: 'for that which is dissolved is devoid of sensation, and that which is devoid of sensation is nothing'.

D: the Demon

The experiment appears in a comment Maxwell wrote to P. G. Tait, the author of *A Sketch of Thermodynamics* (1867). One recent critic, John Maddock, argued in *Nature*, vol. 417 (June 2002) for example not only that the Demon was working by thinking, but that opening and shutting door would have violated the rules of physics too. And anyway, he adds, Maxwell would not have employed a 'demon' as he was a deeply religious man . . . But as for statistical laws, some will also remember reading that the only reason the table does not jump in the air is that it is bound by the sheer unlikeliness of all its molecules choosing to move the same way simultaneously, not by any particular respect for gravity.

Notes and Cuttings

E: Evolution

Darwin, *Origin of Species*, first quote is 193/80, second quote is 176/ 90, and finally 183/117. James Lennox notes these small but significant changes in *Thought Experiments in Science and Philosophy*, edited by Tamara Horowitz and Gerald Massey (Rowman & Littlefield, 1991).

F: the Forms

Plato, Book VI of the *Republic*. The conventional story has just one prisoner escaping to 'see the light' but I'm not sure this evangelical egotism is essential . . . Incidentally, readers (especially students!) are cautioned to read the original too, before committing themselves to any particular view of the philosophers. As I hope can be seen from the 'debates' over even relatively straightforward scenarios like experiment G, second-hand accounts are not worth very much. (Except mine, of course.)

G: Galileo's Balls

Aristotle, *De Caelo*, Book I, vi, 274a.

Galileo, *Discorsi e Dimostrazioni Matematiche* (1628) or Galileo's paper is published in English as *Dialogues Concerning Two Natural Sciences* (Dover, 1954). As noted already, Galileo should not be given too much credit for the experiment, which appears like many other 'Galilean' discoveries to have been borrowed without acknowledgement, in this case from Jan de Groot in 1586. Nonetheless, the style of Galileo's text is unmistakable.

H: Hume's Shades

David Hume, Treatise 1 of *On Human Nature*.

Kuhn writes about thought experiments themselves in a paper: 'A Function for Thought Experiments' published in that auspicious year, 1964, reprinted in *The Essential Tension* (University of Chicago Press, 1977). (See also discussion of probability/possibility in *101 Philosophy Problems* (Routledge, 1999/2002) perhaps.)

I: Identity of Indiscernibles

See Leibniz's *Monadology*, and Wittgenstein's thoughts on the subject in the *Blue and Brown Books* (New York, 1958, pp. 61–2). Newton and Leibniz really were rivals, with Leibniz spending more time belittling Newton's ideas than a truly great philosopher might have been expected to do. In particular Newton's 'occult' notions of 'action at a distance', to accept which Leibniz loftily declared was to 'renounce Philosophy and Reason' and to 'open an asylum for ignorance and laziness'. . .

J: Poincaré's Problem

From 'Space and Geometry', by J. Henri Poincaré, reproduced in *Science and Hypothesis* (Dover, 1952).

K: Kant's Kritik

From the *Critique of Pure Reason* – the Antinomies, this being the second. In words that have a particular resonance for a book on thought experiments (perhaps more so than on the matter at hand), Kant also explains in the preface:

> The brilliant claims of reason striving to extend its dominion beyond the limits of experience, have been represented above only in dry formulae, which contain merely the grounds of its pretensions. They have, besides, in conformity with the character of a transcendental philosophy, been freed from every empirical element; although the full splendour of the promises they hold out, and the anticipations they excite, manifests itself only when in connection with empirical cognitions. In the application of them, however, and in the advancing enlargement of the employment of reason, while struggling to rise from the region of experience and to soar to those sublime ideas, philosophy discovers a value and a dignity, which, if it could but make good its assertions, would raise it far above all other departments of human knowledge – professing, as it does, to present a sure foundation for our highest hopes and the ultimate aims of all the exertions of reason.

Those perhaps previously put off exploring Kant may like to know that there is a new, more accessible translation of the *Kritik*, by George MacDonald Ross, available on the Internet at: http://www.philosophy.leeds.ac.uk/GMR/hmp/modules/kant0203/k0203frame.html.

L: Lucretius' Spear

Lucretius, Book I of *De Rerum Natura*, c.55 BCE. A good translation (and its introduction is very interesting too) is *Lucretius' The Nature of the Universe*, translated by Ronald Latham (Penguin, 1951).

Notes and Cuttings

M: Mach's Motions

Ernst Mach, *The Science of Mechanics*, translated by Thomas McCormack (Open Court, 1960, p. 34).

N: Newton's Bucket

Isaac Newton, Principia II of his *Principia* and also Mach (as above). Newton is less of a thought experimenter than he is a very fastidious observer and mathematician. For instance, using instruments he built and designed himself (as did most of the great scientists then), he plotted the position of the Great Comet of 1680–1 using a ruler and compasses to an accuracy of 0.0017 of an inch. Nonetheless, his enquiring mind swept far beyond narrow definitions of physics or mathematics to also consider questions such as: Why don't the stars themselves fall in one upon each other? How can we explain all the order and beauty of the world? (And when he investigated the Bible he discovered that the invention of Jesus as a 'God' rather than as a human prophet was little more than a case of document forgery . . .) Perhaps, he asked, 'is not infinite Space the Sensorium of a Being incorporeal, living, intelligent, omnipresent?'

O: Olbers' Paradox

For more, see *Darkness at Night: A Riddle of the Universe*, Edward Harrison (Harvard University Press, 1987).

P: Parfit's Person

On the one hand, see Derek Parfit, *Reasons and Persons* (Oxford University Press, 1944). But surprisingly, perhaps, the issue of identity needs to be traced back at least to the Stoic philosopher Chrysippus in Ancient Greece, who offered a thought experiment on it too. This is essentially the template for contemporary philosopher Peter Geach's 'Tibbles the Cat' thought experiment, which runs:

> Suppose that we have a cat named Tibbles. Let us name the part of Tibbles that consists of all of Tibbles but her tail, 'Tib'. Now suppose that at time t, Tibbles meets with an unfortunate accident, and loses her tail (which for clarity let us say is completely destroyed). Tibbles presumably did not cease to exist in this accident, nor did Tib. But after the accident, Tibbles and Tib, distinct material objects, seem to occupy exactly the same region. [!]

Notes and Cuttings

Q: Thought Experiments Quotidiennes

101 Éxperiences de philosophie quotidienne, by Roger-Pol Droit, first published in French by Éditions Odile Jacob in 2001. The English translation, *101 Experiments in the Philosophy of Everyday Life* was published by Faber in 2002.

R: the Rule-ruled Room

See John Searle, 'Minds, Brains and Programs', which is one of a number of essays in a collection by Rainer Born in *Artificial Intelligence: The Case Against* (Croom Helm, 1987), but also perhaps Leibniz's *Monadology* and maybe a smattering of Alan Turing. Daniel Dennett's book, *Consciousness Explained* (Little, Brown & Co., 1991) looks through many brainy thought experiments including the brain in the vat, the brainstorm machine, the colour scientist who has never seen colours, and Searle's Chinese Room. Incidentally, the second interesting question posted into the 'Cruel Room' was once posed by Wittgenstein himself as a sort of 'thought experiment'.

S: Salvatius' Ship

Galileo, *Dialogues Concerning the Two Chief World Systems*, 1632. Christian Huygens developed that theory in *De Motu Corporum ex Percussione*, 1656.

T: The Time-Travelling Twins

Many books talk about time travel, most of them not really as exciting, as they sound, but for instance in *In Search of the Edge of Time* (Penguin, 1995), John Gribbin sets out to explain how time travel is at least theoretically possible and looks at different ways to do so, while in *Black Holes, Wormholes and Time Machines* (Institute of Physics, 1999) J. S. Al-Khalili offers a gentle lead-in to the physics and practicalities.

U: Understanding the Universe

Einstein's intuition quoted in the discussion is from some 'Autobiographical Notes', in *Albert Einstein: Philosopher-Scientist*, edited by A. Schlipp (La Salle, 1949). One of the remarkable effects of relativity is that no matter how many times you read and fully understand the theory – a moment later you have forgotten it all again! So maybe not

Notes and Cuttings

Stephen Hawking . . . Try Nigel Calder, *Einstein's Universe* (Penguin, 1990), or John Gribbin, *Schrödinger's Kittens and the Search for Reality: The Quantum Mysteries Solved* (Phoenix, 1996).

V: the Violinist

Judith Jarvis Thompson, 'A Defense of Abortion', *Philosophy and Public Affairs* (vol. I, no. 1, 1971, pp. 47–66) is the original version of the violinist dilemma. John Finnis followed this up in 1973 with 'The Rights and Wrongs of Abortion: a Reply to Thomson' (*Philosophy and Public Affairs*, vol. 2, no. 2) as did many others, for example, Mary Anne Warren in 'On the Moral and Legal Status of Abortion,' (*Monist*, vol. 57, no. 1, pp. 43–61), where she considers making the victim a volunteer instead.

W: Wittgenstein's Beetle

The beetle lives in Ludwig Wittgenstein, *Philosophical Investigations*, section 293. See also the notes above in the 'How to' guide for further references and reading.

X: Xenophanes

More on Xenophanes in W. K. C. Guthrie's *History of Greek Philosophy* (Cambridge University Press, 1962).

Y: History Counterfactuals

See, for example, *Counterfactual Thought Experiments in World Politics* (Princeton University Press, 1996), a collection of papers edited by Philip Tetlock and Aaron Belkin. Hilary Putnam's book, *Reason, Truth and History* (Cambridge University Press, 1981), also contains an early incarnation of the 'brain-in-a-vat' thought experiment.

Z: Zeno

Not so many books on this great thinker . . . but my *101 Philosophy Problems* (Routledge 1999/2002)has some more on Zeno. See more of Max's theory at: http://www.hep.upenn.edu/-max/multiverse.html.

How to Experiment

The Beetle debate is from:

http://www.bioethics.gov/200209/session4.htm
http://afonasin.chat.ru/wittgenstein.html
http://www.infidels.org/library/modern/james_still/
w_fiction.html
http://www.philosophypages.com/hy/6s.htm by Garth Kemerling
http://www.gustavus.edu/oncampus/academics/philosophy/
Brooke.html [6].

Tamara Horowitz's article discussed was 'Philosophical Intuitions and Psychological Theory', *Ethics* 108, (January 1988, pp. 367–388, and later ruminations can be followed in *Thought Experiments in Science and Philosophy*, edited by Tamara Horowitz, Gerald J. Massey (Rowman & Littlefield, 1993). This sober work contains many relevant articles on the subject in general.

P. F. Strawson wrote in *Individuals, An Essay in Descriptive Metaphysics* (London: Methuen, 1964) and Gareth Evans' response was 'Things Without the Mind: A Commentary upon Chapter Two of Strawson's *Individuals*', *Philosophical Subjects, Essays Presented to P. F. Strawson*, edited by Zak Van Straaten (Clarendon Press, 1980), pp. 76–116. And Wittgenstein's cryptic quote is also one of the *Philosophical Investigations*, paragraph 243.

A Brief 'Who's Who' of Thought Experimentation

ARISTOTLE (384–322 BCE)

Aristotle would happily have discussed all the issues in this book, as his own interests spanned the sciences, mathematics, the arts and, of course, metaphysical speculation. His only mistake was in occasionally using the wrong approach in the wrong area.

EDWARD DE BONO

De Bono being the contemporaneous management guru famous for coining the term 'lateral thinking', whose many books advocate different kinds of thought experiments, but not in our sense so we leave him (other than here) to one side.

CHARLES DARWIN (1809–82)

Darwin is usually considered to have heralded the end of purely intellectual theories (such as that the world was so complicated it must have been designed by God) and the arrival of solid, scrupulously objective empirical research. But as with all great theories, there remained more than a few niggling loose ends that no amount of data collection could quite tidy up . . .

RENÉ DESCARTES (1596–1650)

Descartes, like Darwin rather later, is another thinker credited with 'ushering in' the modern era – and certainly in his mathematical and scientific writings was an original and innovative thinker. However, his famous dictum 'I think, therefore – I am!' was straightforwardly borrowed from his Augustinian teachers, and most of his 'thought experiments' to discover whether the world might be an illusion can be traced back to Plato.

ROGER-POL DROIT

Roger-Pol is the contemporary writer and 'French Philosophe', whose approach is anything but scientific, despite his day-job at the Centre for Scientific Research in Paris . . .

ALBERT EINSTEIN (1879–1955)

Einstein was the Patents Office clerk who made something of a name for himself through speculations on the fundamental nature of the universe. His Theory of Relativity made the speed of light constant and everything else, merely relative.

JOHANN FICHTE (1762–1814)

Not a great thought experimenter, but a German philosophy professor who advocated a kind of 'K for Kantian' view of the world, in which reality is essentially a by-product of thought, a creation of the mind.

GOTTLOB FREGE (1848–1925)

A hard-headed German logician and philosopher of language who – as far as I know – eschewed using the thought experiment technique, advocating instead the supremacy of logic. However, faced by the strange puzzle of the barber who was ordered to cut the hair of all those who do not normally cut their own, as part of a civic drive against unkempt citizens (what was he to do about his own scruffy locks?), he came to see the relevance of the technique. (Bertrand Russell wrote to alert him of the logical conflict – in slightly more precise terms, see below.)

GALILEO GALILEI (1564–1642)

Much of Galileo's most important work was in the form of imaginary experiments, not the result of observations at all – although he was an effective exponent of the 'new technologies' of telescopes and so on too. In actual fact he 'borrowed' many findings – and theories – from other thinkers, and indeed, he is said to have been an insufferably arrogant and vain man. Nonetheless, the fact remains that amongst all the natural philosophers, he is one of the masters of the technique.

CHARLOTTE GILMAN (1860–1935)

As well as editing a newspaper, *The Forerunner*, Charlotte Gilman's study *Women and Economics* (1898), was one of the first to look at the role of women in the economic system, whilst other books such as *Moving the Mountain* in 1911 and *With Her in Ourland* (1916), also used the literary device made famous by Sir Thomas More in describing his 'Utopia'.

DAVID HUME (1711–76)

The Scottish philosopher who held that humans reason rather less than generally supposed (in philosophical circles anyway) and instead merely 'associate' ideas or impressions, either as a matter of accustomed habit, or out of some sort of aesthetic preference for the new arrangement. His *Treatise on Human Nature* (1739) in which the 'Blue Shades' appear was largely ignored on publication, and he miserably described the whole book as falling 'still-born from the press'.

IMMANUEL KANT (1724–1804)

Considered the grittiest if not indeed the greatest of German philosophers, and credited, if you like, with having determined the direction of German philosophy ever since. Our interests here lie with his attempts to define what it is possible to know, but alas his answer is too complicated to follow. In his other other interests – ethics and space-time physics – he was again both innovative and influential, but in these cases, he was definitely wrong. Or as wrong as you can be, in philosophy.

GOTTFRIED LEIBNIZ (1646–1716)

Another obscure and difficult German philosopher, who in this case held that there were two kinds of truth, necessary and, er... unnecessary. Contingent, as philosophers say. The laws of Nature, for example, are one of the latter. They just happen to be true. His principle of the 'Identity of Indiscernibles' (in which two things share the same properties if they are identical) is actually the reverse formulation of an older one suggested by Aristotle, to wit: if two things are identical then they share the same properties. Leibniz also decided that the universe consisted of an infinite number of possible universes filled with an infinite number of identical 'monads' – whatever they are.

ERNST MACH (1836–1913)

Ernst Mach is credited with coining the term 'thought experiment', or to be more precise, *Gedankenexperiment*, and was himself a keen experimenter. As seen already, he was stoutly opposed to metaphysical notions, such as Newton's 'Absolute Space', arguing that science must stick to observable entities, and that as we can only ever ourselves make relative observations – relating our experiences to other ones – the only kind of movement that we can speak of meaningfully is relative motion. Nonetheless, in *The Science of Mechanics*, he set out his view that people all possess a deep reservoir of 'instinctive knowledge' which we can both add to and draw on without being consciously aware of it.

ISAAC NEWTON (1643-1727)

Sir Isaac is sometimes said to have been to science what Euclid was to mathematics. His *Principia* (1686) systematized the science of mechanics, that is the science of objects and how they move, just as Euclid systematized study of geometry. Both provided the terms and definitions for all the rest. Newton found it necessary to deal with otherwise apparently philosophical issues such as those of the nature of 'space' and of 'true motion' (in particular the views of Descartes) in order to address paradoxes such as that of how the Earth could both be 'accelerating' away from the Sun at any moment, and yet be motionless. If his 'Absolute Space' seems to take a bit of a pasting here, it is not to say that the issue is a simple one.

PLATO (427-347 BCE)

Conventionally hailed as the greatest 'systematic' thinker of the Ancient Greeks, although in practice it is difficult to know what he thought, and what he merely reported. Nonetheless, amongst the writings attributed to him are many powerful 'thought experiments', such as Gyges' Ring, the story of the Cave, and so on, and in many ways his dialogues set the parameters for future discussion of this approach, as they do for so many others.

PTOLEMY (87-150 CE)

The Ancient Greek (one who however lived in Egypt) astronomer, mathematician and geographer. His thought experiments may not be much, but his 13-volume book of the heavens, based on at least 80 interacting heavenly spheres, was actually more accurate in calculating positions than the Copernican one that replaced it.

BERTRAND RUSSELL (1872-1970)

Russell was Wittgenstein's tutor and had doubts about his protégé's approach, a compliment returned by Wittgenstein himself. Russell's greatest work was intended to be the creation of a logically rigorous foundation for mathematics, philosophy and science, but it had to be abandoned after the 'discovery' (so to speak) of the paradoxical thought experiment (mentioned above under 'Frege' too) that the set of all sets that are not members of themselves cannot decide whether or not to be a member of itself – or not. It caused him a lot of sleepless nights, as it seemed, at least to him, to leave his grand system in ruins. Happily, however, amongst his many writings are excellent more modest 'thought experiments' such as the Cannibal.

IRWIN SCHRÖDINGER (1887–1961)

Schrödinger's famous cat appeared in a cruel thought experiment in 1935 where it was intended to ridicule the so-called 'Copenhagen Interpretation' in physics, the view which allowed for things to both be and not be, a sort of 'neo-Shakespearean' position.

C. P. SNOW (1905–80)

C. P. Snow is the mid-twentieth-century English writer and scientist whose book *The Two Cultures* warned against science becoming detached from the rest of cultural life. (No one took any notice.)

SOCRATES (469–399 BCE)

Socrates is that enigmatic figure, known best through the writings of Plato, who claims to record his thoughts and views. He seems to have favoured the dialectical method of reasoning, where a view is challenged by offering a contrary, conflicting case. The resolution then has to be a 'synthesis' of the two positions, but this too is then open to challenge. As such, his method is closely related to the thought experiment's one.

LUDWIG WITTGENSTEIN (1889–1951)

And Ludwig Wittgenstein is the *enfant terrible* of thought experimentation, who originally ferociously opposed such attempts to describe the indescribable, but later came to consider the art of communication, let alone philosophy, required such approximations to reality and produced lots of them.

The others mentioned in the text are contemporaneous (or nearly) academics, who have either written on thought experiments or tried a few themselves, including:

James Brown
Daniel Dennett
Brian Ellis
Carol Gilligan
Martin Hollis
Tamara Horowitz
Alisdair McIntyre
John Norton
Warren Quinn
Anthony Quinton
Richard Rorty
John Searle
Peter Strawson
Judith Jarvis Thompson
Bernard Williams

Acknowledgements

A book needs to be the product of two things: inspiration and application. To be sure, many books lack one or the other of these ingredients, but this present work has been lucky in that both inspiration and considerable doses of application have been added to the slightly fetid stew of my initial draft by the excellent Jeff Dean of Blackwell and an ever-expanding circle of consultees and readers. As a result, the paws of my trained typist-labrador, Blackie, have been kept busy over nearly five years now. Not just rewriting experiments to get the 'facts' right, but also rewriting experiments to get the *style* right (which is rather harder).

Whether the book has emerged with flaws or not, is entirely a matter for Blackie, and perhaps the Dog Lovers' Society of America, but I hope the reader will nonetheless appreciate that brevity (as Pascal famously put it) is also the mark of more thought, not less, and certainly that the thought, in this case, has been greatly improved because it has been shared by many others. And so I hope it will continue to be, too.

Martin Cohen
Normandy, France

131

Index

Index

Index

Index